Praise for

DIE WITH

ZERO

A *Wall Street Journal* bestseller

"[T]he ideas contained within are worth pondering for a future that may eventually include a return to a somewhat normal financial life . . . So why is this book by Bill Perkins . . . worth your time? Because it gets to the heart of two extremely important issues that you may be thinking about during these strange times: why you save and how you live . . . It's an intriguing idea."
—*New York Times*

"If you're wondering what the secret sauce is to living your life to the fullest at every stage without running your resources dry, then crack open this practical, timely book."
—Barbara Corcoran, Shark on *Shark Tank* and Founder of The Corcoran Group

"Bill Perkins's *Die with Zero* opens up a completely different avenue of thinking so that your life can be maximized through memorable experiences. Why wait? Being present is a priority. This book provides an amazing blueprint to living your life while using your resources correctly!"
—Kevin Hart, award-winning comedian and actor

"[Bill Perkins is] not offering a steady plan to save for the future while still enjoying your life; he's offering ways to be more present now, so you don't look back on would'ves, could'ves, and should'ves later in life."
—*Success*

DIE WITH
ZERO

DIE PITH

DIE WITH
ZERO

Getting All You Can from Your Money and Your Life

Bill Perkins

MARINER
BOOKS

An Imprint of HarperCollins*Publishers*
Boston   New York

First Mariner Books edition 2021
Copyright © 2020 by William O. Perkins III
Graphics by Charles Denniston. Used by permission.

Mariner Books
An Imprint of HarperCollins Publishers, registered in the United States of America and/or other jurisdictions.

www.marinerbooks.com

Library of Congress Cataloging-in-Publication Data
Names: Perkins, Bill (William O.), 1969– author.
Title: Die with zero : getting all you can from your money and your life /
Bill Perkins.
Description: Boston : Houghton Mifflin Harcourt, 2020. | Includes
bibliographical references and index.
Identifiers: LCCN 2019033906 (print) | LCCN 2019033907 (ebook) |
ISBN 9780358099765 (hardcover) | ISBN 9780358310280 | ISBN 9780358310365 |
ISBN 9780358100515 (ebook) | ISBN 9780358567097 (pbk.)
Subjects: LCSH: Finance, Personal. | Wealth—Psychological aspects. |
Satisfaction.
Classification: LCC HG179 .P3656 2020 (print) | LCC HG179 (ebook) |
DDC 332.024—dc23
LC record available at https://lccn.loc.gov/2019033906
LC ebook record available at https://lccn.loc.gov/2019033907

Book design by Chrissy Kurpeski

Printed in the United States of America
23 24 25 26 27 LBC 12 11 10 9 8

To Skye and Brisa
May you have the fullest lives possible,
full of adventure and love

Contents

Contents

Author's Note

Maybe you've heard the classic Aesop fable of the Ant and the Grasshopper: The industrious ant worked all summer long storing food for the winter, while the carefree grasshopper fiddled and played all summer. So when winter came, the ant was able to survive, while the grasshopper was in dire straits. The moral of the fable? There's a time for work and a time for play.

Great moral. *But when does the ant ever get to play?*

That's the theme of my whole book right there. We know what happens to the grasshopper—the grasshopper starves—but what happens to the ant? That is, if the ant spends his short life slaving away, when does he get to have any fun? We all have to survive, but we all want to do much more than survive: We want to *really live.*

So that's what I focus on in this book: thriving, not just surviving. This book is *not* about making your money grow—it's about making your *life* grow.

I've been thinking about these ideas for years, and arguing about them with friends and colleagues, and now I want to get them out to you. I don't have all the answers, but I do have something here that I know will enrich your life.

I'm not a certified financial planner or a family investment adviser. I'm just somebody who wants to live my life to the fullest, and I want the same for you.

I believe everybody wants that kind of life—but, realistically, not all of us can get it. And just to be up front: If you're struggling to make ends meet, you might get some value out of this book, but not nearly as much as someone with enough money, health, and free time to make real choices about how to put those resources to the greatest use.

So read on. I hope, if nothing else, I get you to reflect and rethink some of your basic assumptions about life.

Bill Perkins
Summer 2019

DIE WITH
ZERO

1

OPTIMIZE YOUR LIFE

Rule No. 1:
Maximize your positive
life experiences.

In October of 2008, Erin and her husband, John, were successful lawyers with three young children when they learned that John had clear-cell sarcoma, a rare and rapidly growing cancer of the body's soft tissues. "Nobody thought that a healthy 35-year-old would have a tumor the size of a baseball," Erin recalls. So no one suspected cancer until the tumor had spread to John's back and leg bones. "We didn't understand how serious his condition was until he had an X-ray and it was lit up like a Christmas tree," Erin says. The grim diagnosis terrified and overwhelmed her. And with John too sick to work, the full burden of taking care of the family physically and financially fell to her. It was too much for one person to bear.

I had been friends with Erin since we were kids, so I wanted to do everything I could to make the situation less horrible. "Stop what you're doing," I told her, "and spend time as a family while John still can." I also offered to help with the costs.

It turns out I was preaching to the choir: Erin had already been thinking about quitting work to focus on what really mattered. And that's what she did. So at their home in Iowa, between John's cancer treatments, the couple enjoyed the simple pleasures of each other's company: They'd go to the park, watch movies, play video games, and pick their kids up after school together.

In November, when local doctors had done everything they could, without success, Erin found a clinical trial in Boston, where she and John made several trips to undergo the experimental treatment, using their free time to go on some of the city's historic tours while John could still walk. All too soon, though, their hope faded, and one day John broke down at the thought of everything he'd miss, from watching his children grow up to passing the years with Erin.

John died in January of 2009, just three months after his diagnosis. Looking back at that period, Erin recalls the trauma and devastation, but she is glad she quit her job to be home with John.

Most people would have done the same in these circumstances. Death wakes people up, and the closer it gets, the more awake and aware we become. When the end is near, we suddenly start thinking, *What the hell am I doing? Why did I wait this long?* Until then, most of us go through life as if we had all the time in the world.

Some of that behavior is rational. It would be foolish to live every day as if it were your last: You wouldn't bother to work, or study for a test, or visit the dentist. So it makes sense to delay gratification to some extent, because that pays off in the long run. But the sad truth is that too many people delay gratification for too long, or indefinitely. They put off what they want to do until it's too late, saving money for experiences they will never enjoy. Living as if your life were infinite is the opposite of taking the long view: It's terribly shortsighted.

Clearly, the story of Erin and John is an extreme case. Advanced clear-cell sarcoma is rare, and death was staring this couple in the face much more starkly than it does for most people. Yet the challenge that their situation presented is common to everyone: Everyone's health generally declines with time, and sooner or later we all die, so the question we all must answer is how to make the most of our finite time on earth.

Put that way, it sounds like a lofty, philosophical question—but that's not how I see it. I'm trained as an engineer and made my fortune on the strength of my analytical skills, so I see this question as an optimization problem: how to maximize fulfillment while minimizing waste.

Everyone's Problem

We all face some version of this question. Of course, the dollar amounts differ from person to person, often dramatically, but the core question is the same for all of us: What's the best way to allocate our life energy before we die?

I have thought about this question for many years, going back to when I was barely earning enough to live on, and over time I've come up with several guiding principles that make sense. These are the ideas behind this book. For example, some experiences can be enjoyed only at certain times: Most people can't go water-skiing in their nineties. Another principle: Although we all have at least the potential to make more money in the future, we can never go back and recapture time that is now gone. So it makes no sense to let opportunities pass us by for fear of squandering our money. Squandering our lives should be a much greater worry.

I'm a big believer in these ideas, and I preach them whenever I get the chance. Whether it's a 25-year-old afraid of pursuing her dream career and instead settling for a safe but soul-crushing job, or a 60-year-old multimillionaire who keeps working long hours in order to sock away more money for retirement instead of enjoying the great wealth he's already accrued, I hate seeing people wasting their resources and putting off living life fully now—and I tell them so. As much as I possibly can, I also practice what I preach. Granted, sometimes I'm like a fat football coach on the sidelines, failing to follow my own advice. But when I catch myself doing that, I make corrections, some of which you'll read about later in this book. None of us are perfect, but I do my best to walk the talk.

We Are All Alike, We Are All Different

Living life fully takes many forms. For example, I love to travel and I love poker, so I take lots of trips, some of them to play in poker tournaments. This means I spend a big percentage of my savings each year on travel and on poker. But don't get me wrong: I am not an advocate for everyone spending their savings on travel, let alone poker. What I *am* an advocate for is deciding what makes you happy and then converting your money into the experiences you choose.

Those enjoyable experiences naturally vary from person to person; some people are active and adventurous, others prefer to stay close to home. Some get great satisfaction from splurging on themselves and their families and friends, while others prefer to spend their time and money on those less fortunate than themselves. And, of course, we can enjoy a mix of experiences. As much as I love to travel, I also like to spend my time and money to advance causes I care about, from railing against bank bailouts to bringing in hurricane relief to my neighbors on the U.S. Virgin Islands. So I'm certainly not trying to tell you that one set of experiences is better than another; instead, you should choose your experiences deliberately and purposefully rather than living life on autopilot, as too many of us do.

Of course, it's more complicated than just knowing what makes you happy and spending your money on those experiences at every moment. That's because our ability to enjoy different kinds of experiences changes throughout our lifetimes. Think about it: If your parents took you along on a tour of Italy when you were a toddler, how much did you get out of that expensive vacation, besides maybe a lifelong love of gelato? Or consider the other extreme: How much do you think you'll enjoy climbing Rome's Spanish Steps when you're in your nineties —assuming you'll still be alive and able to climb them at all by then? As the title of one economics journal article put it, "What Good Is Wealth Without Health?"

In other words, to get the most out of your time and money, timing matters. So to increase your overall lifetime fulfillment, it's important to have each experience at the right age. And that's true no matter what you enjoy or how much money you have. So while the magnitude of everyone's lifetime fulfillment will differ —for example, people with relatively little discretionary income tend to have lower fulfillment levels, and naturally happy people tend to have higher fulfillment levels—we all need to time our experiences properly. Maximizing your fulfillment from experiences—by planning how you will spend your time and money to achieve the biggest peaks you can with the resources you have —is how you maximize your life. By taking charge of these crucial decisions, you take charge of your life.

The Honorary Billionaire

Some of my friends call me an "honorary billionaire," which means exactly what you think it does: I'm not actually a billionaire, but I spend like one.

The reality is, though, that most billionaires won't spend their fortunes during their lifetimes. There's a limit to how much a person can spend on themselves, even with the most lavish tastes, so the ultrawealthy tend to give a lot of money away. Nonetheless, collectively, the 2,000 richest American households (most of them elderly) donate just 1 percent of their total wealth each year, a rate at which they can't possibly use up their vast resources before they die. I'm not talking just about the stingy ultrarich. The richest households also include today's most generous philanthropists—people like Bill Gates, Warren Buffett, and Michael Bloomberg, all of whom have pledged to give their fortunes away. Yet even these extraordinary donors have trouble spending their billions fast enough. That's partly because they've amassed so much wealth that their money is growing more each year than they're able to give away in a thoughtful, responsible way. Gates, for example, has seen his wealth almost double since 2010 — even as he's been devoting himself to fighting disease and poverty. Though I hate to pick on someone who's doing so much amazing good in the world, I have to wonder how much more Gates's immense fortune could do if he managed to deploy it right now!

At least Gates had the wisdom and foresight to stop working for money when he was still young enough to start spending it in a big way. Too many wealthy, successful people fail to do that. And even Gates should have retired from paying work sooner, before accumulating several times what he could spend in one lifetime. Life is not a game of *Space Invaders* — you don't get points for all the money you rack up in the game — but many people treat it as though it were. They just keep earning and earning, trying to maximize their wealth without giving nearly as much thought to maximizing what they get out of that wealth — including what they can give to their children, their friends, and the larger society now, instead of waiting until they die.

A Life-Changing Conversation

I didn't always think this way, and definitely not when I was working my first job after college. At the University of Iowa, I'd played football and majored in electrical engineering. Even though I loved engineering and still have that optimizing mindset, I knew by the time job recruiters came to campus that there was just no way I would pursue the typical engineering career path. Working for a company like, say, IBM, it would take me years of work on a subsection of a subsection of a chip to get a chance to do any actual design. That didn't seem exciting. The rigid schedule—and with only a couple of weeks of vacation each year—would get in the way of all the other things I wanted to do. To be sure, I was young and had delusions of grandeur. But I was certain there was something much better out there for me.

The movie *Wall Street* had come out when I was in college. Today most people kind of laugh at that movie: We deride the slick-haired Michael Douglas character, Gordon Gekko, who told us that "greed, for want of a better word, is good." We all know where that kind of unbridled capitalism got our country. But at the time, the rich and freewheeling lifestyle that the movie portrayed really appealed to me. I sensed that the financial industry would give me the kind of freedom I wanted.

So I took a job on the floor of the New York Mercantile Exchange. My title was "screen clerk"—I was an assistant peon, doing things like sneaking sandwiches for my bosses onto the trading floor. It was the finance industry's equivalent of working in the mail room in Hollywood.

My salary in that job started at $16,000 a year—not exactly enough to live on in New York City, even back in the early 1990s —so I moved back home with my mom in Orange, New Jersey. After I'd gotten promoted to "head screen clerk" and was earning $18,000, I was able to move to Manhattan's Upper West Side by sharing a studio apartment. My roommate and I put up a makeshift wall that gave me a quasi-bedroom the size of a pizza oven. I had so little disposable income in those days that if I didn't buy a monthly subway pass, I was busted because I couldn't afford full fare on a daily basis. When I'd take a date out to the movies, I'd be sweating bullets if she ordered a popcorn. Seriously.

So I started driving my boss's limo at night to earn extra cash. And I became super-thrifty, trying to sock away as much savings as I could. The only guy I knew who was cheaper than me was my friend Tony, who would scrounge up the unpopped kernels from a bowl of popcorn so he could reuse them later, after refrigerating them in the hope of getting their moisture back.

I was proud of my thriftiness, really pleased with myself for managing to save money on such a low income. Then, one day, I was talking to my boss, Joe Farrell, a partner at the company I was working for, and somehow we got to talking about my savings. I told him how much I had saved up—I think it was about $1,000 by then—thinking he would admire my money management skills. Boy, was I wrong! This was his infamous response:

"Are you a f***ing idiot? To save that money?"

It was like a slap across my face. He went on. "You came here to make *millions*," he said. "Your earning power is going to happen! Do you think you'll only make 18 thousand a year for the rest of your life?"

He was right. I hadn't taken a job on Wall Street to make so little, and I would almost certainly earn more in the years to come. So why should I save this random percentage of my modest income for the future? I should enjoy that measly $1,000 right now!

It was a life-changing moment—it just cracked my head open to new ideas about how to balance your earnings with your spending. I didn't know it at the time, but what Joe Farrell was talking about is actually a pretty old idea in finance and accounting. It's called *consumption smoothing*. Our incomes might vary from one month or one year to another, but that doesn't mean our spending should reflect those variations—we would be better off if we evened out those variations. To do that, we need to basically transfer money from years of abundance into the leaner years. That's one use of savings accounts. But in my case, I had been using my savings account totally backwards—I was taking money away from my starving younger self to give to my future wealthier self! No wonder Joe called me an idiot.

Reading this today, you might be saying: Okay, consumption smoothing makes sense in theory, but how could you really know that you would be so much wealthier in the future than you were then? Not every screen clerk goes on to become a successful trader, any more than every kid in a Hollywood mail room becomes a studio mogul. It's a fair question, and I'm the first to admit that a lot of things had to go right for me to get where I am today. It's true that I couldn't predict the *magnitude* of my future earnings. But here's the thing: I was right to be confident of the *direction* of my earnings. I couldn't know I would go on to earn millions, but I sure knew I'd be making more than $18,000 a year! In fact, I could have waited tables and earned more.

Your Money or Your Life

Right around this time, I came across an important and influential book: *Your Money or Your Life,* by Vicki Robins and Joe Dominguez. That book, which I've reread several times since —and which, about 25 years later, is now popular with a new generation of readers, many of whom are part of the FIRE movement ("financial independence, retire early")—completely transformed my understanding of the value of my time and my life: I realized from reading that book that I was wasting valuable hours of my life.

How? The book contended that your money represents life energy. *Life energy* is all the hours that you're alive to do things —and whenever you work, you spend some of that finite life energy. So any amount of money you've earned through your work represents the amount of life energy you spent earning that money. That is true regardless of how much or how little your work pays. So even if you're earning only $8 an hour, spending that $8 also means spending an hour's worth of your life energy. That simple idea made a huge impact on me, hitting me much harder than the old cliché that time is money. I started to think, *You're taking my life energy and you're giving me paper!* It was like the end of *The Matrix,* when Neo walks around seeing the world as it is. That's how I was after reading the book: I started going around calculating hours needed to buy stuff. I'd see a nice-looking shirt, do the mental math, and think, *No, you cannot get me to work two hours just to buy that shirt!*

Several other ideas from that book stayed with me, but I'll just share the one most relevant to the pages you're reading right now: A higher salary doesn't always mean more actual income on an hourly basis. For example, a person making $40,000 per year might actually be making more per hour than someone earning $70,000 per year. How is that possible? Again, it's all about life energy. If the $70,000 job costs you more in terms of your life energy—the cost in time of a long commute to the city, the cost of the kinds of clothes you need for this high-status job, and of course the extra hours you have to put into the job itself—then the person making the higher salary often comes out poorer in the end. This supposedly high earner also has less time left to enjoy the money he or she is earning. So when you're comparing jobs, you really have to factor in those hidden but essential costs.

For me, it comes down to cookies. For the sake of the cartilage between my knees and for other health reasons, I like to maintain a certain body weight, so when I look at a cookie, I convert it to time on the treadmill. Sometimes, when I see a cookie that looks good, I'll take a bite to see how good it tastes and then ask myself, *Is eating this cookie worth walking an extra hour on the treadmill?* The answer is not always no (although it usually is), but either way, it's never a thoughtless decision. These kinds of calculations—whether with money and time, or food and exercise—help us be more deliberate in our choices, which ultimately means we're making better choices than if we act from impulse or out of habit.

I'm not saying that all work—or all workouts—are a time sink. You probably enjoy aspects of your job; in fact, you might be happy to do some of it even if you weren't getting paid. But that's the smallest part of most people's jobs: If we didn't have to work to earn money, most of us would find other things we'd much rather do with our time.

As Americans, we're steeped in the old-fashioned work ethic. But people in many other cultures understand that life is about much more than work. You get a sense of that from the amount of yearly paid vacation time people in many European countries take—six weeks or more in places like France and Germany! On the island of St. Barts, one of my favorite places on the planet, every shop closes for two hours in the middle of the day so that everyone can hang out with their friends and enjoy a nice long lunch. That's a much better work-life balance than most of us are used to.

Your Life Is the Sum of
Your Experiences

And that's also very much in the spirit of *Your Money or Your Life*. Above all, the authors of that book urge us not to sacrifice our lives for money; they want us not to be slaves to our jobs and our possessions. So how do they suggest we go about achieving this financial freedom? The path they lay out is frugality—choosing to live simply so that you don't *need* a lot of money. Yet that's *not* one of my big takeaways from their life-changing book, and it's not what I'm advocating for you.

Instead, I'm a big believer in the value of experiences. Experiences don't have to cost a lot of money, and they can even be free, but worthwhile experiences do usually cost some money. The unforgettable trip, the concert tickets, the pursuit of an entrepreneurial dream or a new hobby—all these experiences cost money, and sometimes they cost a lot of money. To me, that is money well worth spending. Many psychological studies have shown that spending money on experiences makes us happier than spending money on *things*. Unlike material possessions, which seem exciting at the beginning but then often depreciate quickly, experiences actually gain in value over time: They pay what I call a *memory dividend,* which you'll read a lot more about in the next chapter. Living on a shoestring when you can afford more deprives you of those experiences and makes your world smaller than it needs to be.

So your life is the sum of your experiences. But how do you maximize the value of your experiences in order to make the most out of your one life? Or, as I put it earlier in this chapter: What's the best way to spend your life energy before you die?

This book is my answer to that question.

Why This Book

This book started out as an app. I knew there had to be an optimal way to spend your life energy, and that most people were doing it suboptimally. Part of the reason is the complexity of the math: As humans, we have trouble processing large amounts of data involving multiple variables, and when we get overwhelmed we go on autopilot, and the result is far from optimal. Computers are much better at solving these sorts of problems. So I figured I'd create an app that helps people optimize their lives, or at least gets as close as a person and a computer reasonably can.

Then, a few years ago, I was talking to my doctor—one of these doctors in L.A. who basically tries to keep you alive forever. His name is Chris Renna and he works at a clinic called Life-Span that does super-comprehensive testing to catch problems early. The earlier you catch medical problems, the greater your odds of not only avoiding calamity but also having a healthier life. For example, if you have something torn and you avoid tearing it more, you're going to have a better quality of life. So he was asking me all kinds of questions to catch medical concerns early. Questions like "Do you get seven hours of sleep?" "How's your love life?" "Do you have any problems peeing?" Everything you could ask. And then, as part of the psychological evaluation, he asked a question about financial stress: "Do you have fears of running out of money?"

I said, "I *hope* I run out of money!"

He gave me a puzzled look. So I went into my whole spiel about wanting a life full of experiences, and how I won't be able to use my money when I'm dead or too old for many experiences, and that therefore I should aim to die with zero.

He said nobody had ever answered the question that way. Even though his patients are typically wealthy, many of them still have fears of running out of money. I told him I was working on an app to help people with that problem, and he said, "No, you have to write a book. You have to get out there and tell the whole story—explain all your concepts, and not just to users of the app. And you have to start now." He even introduced me to some ghostwriters!

But the book you're reading now isn't exactly the book Dr. Renna had in mind. It turns out that what most excited him—the novelty of explaining why you should die with zero—was also what turned many people off. Wealthy people obviously aren't the only ones afraid of running out of money: It's a fear I heard about over and over from people who'd heard my ideas. So you'll see me addressing this fear throughout the book. After all, nobody would ever try to die with zero if they're afraid they'll hit zero *before* they die.

I want to be clear, though, that not all financial fears are the same. Some people's fears are irrational: They have plenty of resources, so if they plan right, they won't need to worry about running out of money. Those are the people I'm writing for—people who are saving too much for their own good. But for millions of Americans, and billions more living outside this country, the fear of running out of money is more than just a fear. The poorest among us, unfortunately, are in that boat: If you have little or no discretionary income, then by definition you have very little choice in how to spend your money, and so it makes perfect sense for you to focus on surviving. The indigent just don't have the luxury of trying to find the optimal balance between work and play, or between spending now and investing for the future. Within the constraints of their dire circumstances, people in poverty are probably already doing all they can to get the most out of their money and their life.

The fear of running out of money is also reasonable for freewheeling spenders: These are people who really *are* spending too much too soon, so they *should* be afraid! I want to turn the fable of the Ant and the Grasshopper upside down, to show people that delaying gratification at the extreme means no gratification—but I'm also fully aware that, unfortunately, many people identify with the grasshopper all too well.

To some extent, this book is for both sides. Whether you're Sue Spendy, sacrificing future experiences that you didn't even know you wanted to have, or you're Joe Nose-to-the-Grindstone, still going to work doing something that you don't like just so you can earn money for experiences you're never going to have, you're living suboptimally. That said, this book is much more about dragging the ant toward the grasshopper than the other way around.

There are many ways to be suboptimal and only one way to be perfectly optimal. None of us will ever be perfect, but by following the principles in this book, you will avoid the most egregious errors and get more out of your money and your life.

How? All living things, including humans, are energy-processing units. We process food so we can power our bodies. Processing energy lets us not only survive on earth but also live a potentially fulfilling life: With that energy, we can move about the world. Movement is life, and as we move we get continuous feedback—which leads to discovery, wonder, joy, and all the other experiences you can have throughout life's great adventure. When you are no longer able to process energy, you will be declared dead and your adventure will be over. This book is about making the most of your adventure before it ends. Since the reward of processing energy is the experiences that you get to choose, it stands to reason that the way to make the most of your life is to maximize the number of these life experiences—particularly positive ones.

But that probably makes the maximization challenge sound easier than it actually is. To make the most of your life, you can't just start grabbing as many positive life experiences as you're able to find. That's because most experiences cost money. (For starters, the food that gives you life energy most certainly isn't free.) So although it would be super-efficient to convert all of your life energy directly into experiences, you often have to take the intermediate step of earning money. In other words, you have to spend at least some amount of your life energy working—then using your earnings to gain experiences.

But when your goal is to maximize fulfillment across your life span, it's not at all obvious how much of your life energy should be applied to earning money (and when) and how much to having experiences. For one thing, everybody is different in several important ways—there are just a lot of variables to consider. So this turns out to be a complex optimization problem. That's why an app is useful—it can take in many variables and do the calculations necessary to help you compare different possible life paths, showing which path leads to more fulfillment. Yet even an app can't optimize perfectly, because even the most sophisticated model can't fully capture the complexity of a human life; also, an app's results are only as good as the data it's given, most of which isn't perfect, either. Still, with or without software, it's possible to think intelligently about these earning and spending decisions. And although I don't have all the answers, and never will, I'm confident of the guiding principles I mentioned earlier, along with several others. Each chapter in this book explains one of these principles, or "rules," that lead to wiser decisions about allocating your precious life energy. You and I will never achieve perfection, but by applying these rules to your own life you'll be able to move closer to that optimal point.

My overarching goal is to get you to think about your life in a more purposeful, deliberate manner, instead of simply doing things as you and others have always done them. Yes, I want you to plan for your future—but never in such a way that you forget to enjoy the present. We all get one ride on this roller coaster of life. Let's start thinking about how to make it the most exciting, exhilarating, and satisfying ride it can be.

Recommendation

Start actively thinking about the life experiences you'd like to have, and the number of times you'd like to have them. The experiences can be large or small, free or costly, charitable or hedonistic. But think about what you really want out of this life in terms of meaningful and memorable experiences.

2

INVEST IN EXPERIENCES

Rule No. 2:
Start investing in experiences early.

When I was in my early twenties, my roommate at the time, Jason Ruffo, decided to take about three months off from work to go on a backpacking trip to Europe. This is the same friend with whom I was splitting the rent on a pizza-oven-size apartment in Manhattan: We were both screen clerks making about $18,000 a year.

To make a trip like that a reality, Jason would have to put his job on hold—and he'd have to borrow about ten grand from the only person who would lend him that much money: a loan shark. You know, the kind of lender who doesn't ask for collateral and doesn't care about your credit report because he has other ways to make sure you pay up.

I said to Jason, "Are you crazy? Borrowing money from a loan shark? You'll get your legs broken!" I wasn't worried only about Jason's physical safety. Going off to Europe meant that Jason would also miss out on opportunities for advancement in his job. To me, the idea of doing something like that was as foreign as going to the moon. No way was I going to go with him.

But Jason was determined, so off he flew to London, both nervous and excited about traveling alone with a Eurail pass and no set schedule. When he came back a few months later, there was no discernible difference between his income and mine—but the pictures and stories of his experiences showed that he was infinitely richer for having gone. You have to remember: This was the early 1990s, before high-speed Internet and Google Earth. To see what Prague looked like without actually going, you had to get a coffee-table photo book about the place. So hearing his stories and looking at his photos was like listening to some exotic explorer.

In Germany, he saw the horrors of Dachau. In the newly formed Czech Republic, he heard about life under Communist rule. In Paris, he and two friends he'd made whiled away an afternoon sitting in a park, just enjoying baguettes with cheese and wine and feeling like anything was possible. Eventually he made his way to the Greek islands. Somewhere along the way he fell in love with a woman and had sex on a beach for the first time. As he met locals and young travelers from all over, he learned more about himself and other people and cultures and felt his world opening up. His stories of the interesting cultures he'd seen and the connections he had made were so amazing, I felt pretty envious—and regretful that I hadn't gone.

As time passed, that feeling of regret only grew. When I finally went to Europe, at age 30, it was too late: I was already a tad too old and too bougie to stay in youth hostels and hang out with a bunch of 24-year-olds. Plus, by the time I was 30, I had many more responsibilities than I'd had in my early twenties, which made it that much harder to take months off for travel. I finally, unfortunately, had to conclude that I should have just gone earlier.

Like me, Jason knows he timed that European trip exactly right. "I wouldn't enjoy sleeping in a youth hostel with 20 guys on a shitty bunk bed now, and I wouldn't enjoy carrying a 60-pound backpack around on trains and through the streets."

But unlike me, he actually took the trip, so he doesn't have to live with second thoughts. In fact, despite the high-interest loan, he has the opposite of regret about the expense. "Whatever I paid, I feel it was a bargain because of the life experiences I gained," he tells me. "You can't take those away, and I would never have them erased for any amount of money." What he gained from that trip, in other words, is priceless.

Back when Jason first decided to take that trip, he was flying by the seat of his pants. He wasn't planning out his whole life and consciously deciding to *invest in experiences* when he was young. In a way, he was lucky that his instincts led him to such a great decision. But more typically, instincts aren't enough, and they often steer us the wrong way. My aim throughout this book, on the other hand, is to make you much more deliberate in your life choices—to use data and reason to figure out what to do. That's how you'll make the best decisions. And in this chapter, that means showing you how to think about your life experiences in a more quantitative way than you're probably used to ever doing.

The Business of Your Life

The main idea here is that your life is the sum of your experiences. This just means that everything you do in life—all the daily, weekly, monthly, annual, and once-in-a-lifetime experiences you have—adds up to who you are. When you look back on your life, the richness of those experiences will determine your judgment of how full a life you've led. So it stands to reason that you should put some serious thought and effort into planning the kinds of experiences that you want for yourself. Without that kind of deliberate planning, you're bound to just follow our culture's well-trodden, default path through life—to coast on autopilot. You'll get to your destination (death) but probably without having the kind of journey you would have actively chosen for yourself.

Sadly, that is how too many people spend their lives. To switch metaphors: They build a well, they get a pump, and as the pump pumps water into a cup, the cup quickly fills, so the water starts overflowing. They take a sip and they keep pumping. And at the end of their lives, after a lifetime of pumping, they see that they're still thirsty. What a waste! Imagine the regret you would feel if you got to the end of your days only to realize you haven't managed to live a life full of satisfying experiences. In the wise words of Carson, the butler of *Downton Abbey*, "The business of life is the acquisition of memories. In the end that's all there is."

That sounds really nice, but it's also the sort of thought that tends to go in one ear and out the other. You hear it, maybe nod approvingly, and then go back to business as usual. Toward the end of my father's life, though, this idea that life is about acquiring memories really hit home.

Dad could not have enjoyed any kind of vacation at that point — his physical ability was greatly diminished, and travel would have posed too great a risk to his life. Instead I gave him a shamelessly sentimental gift: an iPad full of memories. As a college student, he had played football for several seasons at the University of Iowa in the early 1960s. So I took a highlight reel from that glorious season, had it digitized, and put it on the iPad. We're always reliving parts of our lives through memories, and I figured that this format would make the memories more vivid and easily accessible to him. Sure enough, he loved it. As he sat holding the iPad and watching the video, he laughed, he cried, he reminisced. Too old to acquire significant new experiences, he could still derive great enjoyment from the highlight video. In fact, he thought it was the best gift ever. That was when I realized that you *retire on your memories.* When you're too frail to do much of anything else, you can still look back on the life you've lived and experience immense pride, joy, and the bittersweet feeling of nostalgia.

Between the Ant and the Grasshopper

The idea that you retire on your memories runs completely counter to most of what we normally hear about retirement. As workers in the United States, we're constantly getting the message that we must save for retirement, that we need to regularly sock money away into a 401(k) plan or IRA. That's just the grown-up version of lessons we learned as kids about the need to save for a rainy day.

The best-remembered variant of the fable of the Ant and the Grasshopper, for example, has the ant sitting pretty (and pretty smug) after harvesting his grain, while the grasshopper goes hungry after spending his whole summer playing. That retelling leaves no doubt about which of the two insects had done the right thing, and it sure wasn't the fun-loving, shortsighted grasshopper.

But don't get me wrong: My point isn't that we should be just like the grasshopper, failing to save for the winter of our life, or that any amount we spend on experiences is worth it because experiences are the stuff of life. That would be foolish. What I'm saying is that our culture tends to *overemphasize* the virtues of the ant—of hard work and delayed gratification—at the cost of other virtues. As a result, we fail to appreciate that the grasshopper was onto something, too. So, yes, the grasshopper would be better off to save a little—and, yes, the ant would be better off to live a little! I'm here to bridge the ant and the grasshopper, to help you find the right balance between the two. In fact, the stated moral of my favorite version of the fable is just this: "There is a time for work and a time for play." In a later chapter, I will present actual tools to help you figure out the right time (and the right amount of time) for work and for play—for earning money and for spending it.

What's an Experience Worth?

Earlier I said that life is the sum of all experiences. Well, I wasn't just speaking figuratively: If you were to put a numerical value on each experience, you could then actually add up the value of multiple experiences. Doing that makes it possible to compare bundles of disparate experiences, which is a step toward maximizing your lifetime fulfillment.

How do you place a numerical value on an experience? For starters, think about the enjoyment you get from each experience in terms of points, like the points you'd earn in a game. Peak experiences will bring you many *experience points*. Small pleasures will get only a few points. How many points you assign to an activity is totally up to you, because everybody's values and interests are different. Some people like nothing more than tending their garden, so they would say that every day they spend gardening gets a high number of points. Other people would say you'd have to *pay* them to prune plants or pull weeds, so for them any time spent gardening would get zero points. (There are no negative points in this system.)

If you take all of your positive experiences from a given year —say, last year—and add up their point values, you get a number (for example, 5,090 points). You can represent this number as a bar on a bar chart. The higher the number, the higher the bar. It's as simple as that.

You can do the same for every year of your life so far. Some years are better than others, for various reasons, and some of these reasons are out of your control. (If an accident left you confined to a hospital bed for 12 months, for example, you probably wouldn't have many enjoyable experiences that year.) But this book focuses on managing what *is* under your control through the decisions you make—so realize that a few factors are in your control, and one of the biggest is how much time at each age you devote to earning money versus having enjoyable experiences. It's just like the work-play trade-off faced by the ant and the grasshopper. As you take control of these decisions, you

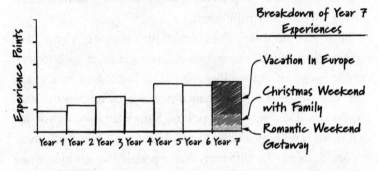

Example of a Fulfillment Curve for a 7-Year Period

Each bar represents the number of experience points for one year. All the bars together help make up your fulfillment curve. So increasing your total fulfillment increases the area under the curve—and by shaping the curve, you shape your life.

change the heights of the bars and therefore the shape of your curve. We'll talk more about how to make these trade-offs later —for now, I just want you to understand that I literally mean that life is the sum of your experiences.

The Memory Dividend

This chapter tells you to invest in experiences—but are experiences really an investment? I mean, it's easy to see that experiences take time and money, and that they can bring enjoyment during the days and years you are having those experiences, which makes them worthwhile for that reason alone. But let me tell you why I say that they're also an investment in your future.

First, let's talk about what an investment is. Most of us hear that word and right away think of the stock market. Or bonds.

Or a portfolio of different investments, such as stocks, bonds, and real estate. What do all investments have in common? They are just mechanisms for generating future income. When you buy stock in, say, IBM, you are hoping that you will be able to sell the stock later for more than you bought it for or at least be able to earn dividends that IBM issues to shareholders, a teeny-tiny fraction of the company's profits every year. Are you with me so far? The same with real estate: You buy a house that you think you can resell for a profit in a few years, and in the meantime you can rent it out and generate passive income every month, as long as your tenants pay the rent. If you own a business that makes widgets, and you buy a new machine that will crank out widgets twice as fast, with fewer defects, then the new machine is an investment in your business.

Standard, right? Now think about how to extend this idea, which we do all the time without necessarily thinking about it in terms of investment. For example, let's say you're a parent paying for your kid to go to college or graduate school. Why are you paying tens of thousands each year? Because you think it's worth it. You probably believe your son or daughter will graduate with the kinds of skills and degree that will help them earn a much higher income than they would without the university education. But maybe you're skeptical that their degree will ever pay off: Let's say your son wants to study Himalayan basket weaving, and you hear that robots are getting so good at making baskets that all those lucrative basket-weaving jobs are disappearing. In that case, you will probably be a lot less eager to write the big checks to the university. When you're thinking about these things, you are making investment decisions just as surely as if you were looking at rental properties or factory machines to buy. Economists even call expenditures on education "investment in human capital."

So you see that you can invest in yourself or in other people. You do this whenever you think the investment will pay off in the future. Now, here's a more radical idea: The payoff from an investment does not have to be financial. When you teach your daughter to swim or to ride a bike, it's not because you think she'll get a better-paying job with those new skills. Experiences are like that: When you spend time or money on experiences, they are not only enjoyable in the moment—they pay an ongoing dividend, the memory dividend I mentioned in chapter 1.

Experiences yield dividends because we humans have memory. We don't start every day with a blank brain, like characters in so many sci-fi movies. We wake up every morning preloaded with a bunch of memories that we can access at any time—mainly to get around and navigate the world. When you face a large rectangular panel with a protruding round knob, you don't ask yourself, *What is this thing?* No, you know it's a door. And you know how to open that door. So there's a huge dividend from having once learned what a door is—think of all the doors you can open!

That's a silly example, but it really shows what memories do for us. They are an investment in our future selves, paying dividends and helping us live richer lives. You see the person making coffee in your kitchen and you don't start from scratch with them, as if you're meeting a stranger. You know this is a person you love, and you know why you love this person. All the history that went into your relationship, all your past conversations and shared experiences, built the current feeling you have toward this person.

It's the same thing when you're investing in any experience. When you have an experience, you get that current, in-the-moment enjoyment, but you also form memories that you get to relive later. This is a big part of being present as a living human being: For better or worse, you re-experience that experience, often more than once. You might hear a favorite song, get a whiff of a familiar scent, look at an old photo, and suddenly your memory's triggered and you are reliving that experience. You think of your first kiss, and if that was a pleasant experience, then you might feel warm and fuzzy. Or you might chuckle because you had braces and the whole experience was embarrassing but also sweet. So every time you remember the original experience, you get an additional experience from mentally and emotionally reliving the original experience.

The recollection may bring you just a tiny fraction of the enjoyment that the original experience did, but those memories add up to make you who you are. That's why Jason, whose story I opened this chapter with, wouldn't erase his backpacking trip through Europe for anything. It's also why people keep photo albums—and why, if their house is on fire, they usually grab their albums before trying to save just about any other possession. In that moment of crisis, people quickly realize that, whereas material objects can be replaced, memories are priceless.

The memory dividend is so powerful and valuable that tech companies are monetizing it and creating billions in wealth. Anyone who's used Facebook or Google Photos has seen the occasional "On this day 3 years ago" message, with accompanying photos from that day. Through this feature, the companies tap into your memory dividend, sparking good feelings and a desire to reach out to those included in the photos. This whole process makes you happy—and makes you a more loyal customer. Before Facebook and the like, it used to be our friends and family who'd spark the "remember when" conversation—but now FB plays that role and cashes in financially on that all-important memory dividend. You can cash in on the memory dividend yourself, non-financially—but to do that, you first need to create those valuable memories.

Think back to one of the best vacations you ever had, and let's say it lasted a full week. Now think about how much time you spent showing pictures of that trip to your friends back home. Add to that all the times you and the people you traveled with reminisced about that trip, and all the times you've thought about it yourself or given advice to other people considering going on a similar trip. All those residual experiences from the original experience are the dividends I'm talking about—they're your memory dividends, and they add up. In fact, some of these memories, upon repeat reflection, may actually bring more enjoyment than the original experience itself.

So buying an experience doesn't just buy you the experience itself—it also buys you the sum of all the dividends that experience will bring for the rest of your life.

This becomes really clear when you think in terms of experience points—my way of quantifying how much enjoyment you got out of an experience. Remember how you can represent the number of experience points with a vertical bar? Okay, now think about that bar as just the beginning of the enjoyment you are getting from the experience. Because of the memory dividend, you also receive an additional little bar every time you recall the original experience. If you stack up all those little bars —all the ongoing memory dividends from an experience—you get a second bar that might be as tall as the bar that represents the original experience.

In fact, sometimes the second bar is even taller. One way this can happen is through compounding, just like with money in the bank. Due to compounding, your financial savings don't just

Example of a 7-Year Fulfillment Curve with Memory Dividends

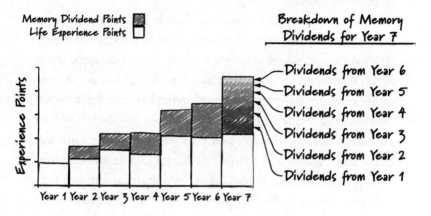

Experiences keep on giving in the form of fulfillment from your memories: Over time, the ongoing memory dividend can sometimes add up to more experience points than the original experience provided.

add up—they begin to snowball. And the same thing can happen with your memory dividends—they also can and will compound. This happens whenever you share the memory of the experience with other people. That's because whenever you interact with someone, sharing an experience you've had, that is an experience in itself. You're communicating, laughing, bonding, giving advice, helping them, being vulnerable—you're doing the stuff of everyday life. By having experiences, you not only live a more engaged and interesting life yourself, but you also have more of yourself to share with others. It's like the idea that business begets more business. Positive experiences are radioactive and contagious in a good way; they start a chain reaction that releases more energy than you thought you had. One plus one can be more than two. That's one of the reasons I say that you should invest in experiences.

But most of us are not used to thinking about investing in experiences—so if we are investors at all, we focus too much on the financial payoff of an investment. A good example is my friend Paulie, who a while back asked me for advice about a vacation property he was considering buying in Central America. I won't bore you with the financial gobbledygook—he was weighing things like interest rates and tax breaks and other considerations that made it all seem like a difficult investment decision. I will just say that he was looking at the opportunity from a very conservative and traditional point of view: *Is this a good real estate investment, meaning will I get a good financial return on it over the next 10 to 15 years?*

My advice to my friend was to reject that whole framework. "Forget the money," I told him, "and let's just talk about what you're going to get out of it. You're my age," I reminded him (no spring chicken). "So how much are you going to use this property to invest in your own personal experiences—how often do you plan to stay there, and what will you do when you're there? If you're going to go there many times and you're going to have wonderful vacations and bond with your kids and have irreplaceable moments with your family and friends, well, that sounds like the greatest deal on planet Earth to me!"

I went on: "But if you're just going to buy the property and have it sit there doing nothing but appreciating your capital investment, then who cares if you stand to gain an extra 3 percent on it? There is nothing special or life-changing about earning 3 percent on foreign real estate—it's just one of a million types of investments you could make. That extra 3 percent is especially insignificant when you start at age 50, as compared with starting much earlier. Investing in experiences, on the other hand, really could change your life, even at 50."

My point to you is that, like so many people who invest in real estate, Paulie was thinking only about return on equity—not about return on experience. To me that's just another version of the same mistake I'm always harping about: earning and earning while forgetting that your whole point in earning money is to be able to spend it on the experiences that make your life what it is.

Think about it: Whether the experiences we want are learning, skiing, watching our children grow, traveling, enjoying great meals with friends, advancing a political cause, attending live concerts, or any of the trillions of combinations of experiences available to us, we acquire money with the goal of having experiences. Plus, because of the memory dividend, those experiences bring some rate of return, just as investments in financial instruments do—sometimes a ridiculously high rate of return. This is what Jason was talking about when he said that he would not trade his European experiences for any amount of money. Of course, most experiences won't be as life-changing as Jason's were, so they won't bring as impressive a rate of return—and they don't have to. We get a return on all our experiences. That's why we spend money on them. It is also why we invest in financial instruments—to help our money grow, with the ultimate goal of generating more or better experiences.

Yet again—and I can't say this enough—many people live as if they forget that this is the point of earning, saving, and investing money. When you ask people what they're saving money for, much of the time the answer is "retirement." To some extent, I get it: We all need to save and invest some amount of money for a time when we're no longer getting a paycheck. Nobody wants to starve in their old age or make their children have to support them. But here's the thing: Since the whole point of money is to have experiences, investing money to get a return with which to have experiences is a roundabout way of having experiences. Why go through all that when you can just invest directly in experiences—and get a return on experiences? Not only that, but the number of actual experiences available to you diminishes as you age. Yes, you need money to survive in retirement, but the *main thing* you'll be retiring on will be your memories—so make sure you invest enough in those.

Start Early, Start Early, Start Early

Once you start thinking about the memory dividend, something becomes really clear: It pays to invest early. The earlier you start investing, the more time you have to reap your memory dividends. For example, if you start in your twenties (rather than your thirties), you'll have a long tail of memory dividends—so you'll be more likely to have the tail add up to more than the head (the number of experience points from the initial event). Clearly, the closer you are to death when you start having wonderful experiences, the fewer memory dividends you will have.

So when I say you should invest in experiences, my investment advice is pretty much standard. It's kind of like what Warren Buffett says: Invest early, and by the time you get to a certain age, look at how much you've accumulated. Many investment advisers want you to start your 401(k) plan early. A lot of investment advice is like that: *Start early, start early, start early.* Warren Buffett and other investment advisers are trying to grow money, and I'm trying to grow the richest life I can; and when I say rich,

I mean rich in experiences, in adventures, in memories—rich in all the reasons you acquire money. So here's my investment advice in a nutshell: Invest in your life's experiences—and start early, start early, start early.

Now, you might be saying, how can you expect me to invest in experiences early in life when I'm broke? But investing in experiences doesn't mean spending money you don't have. It's true that, in general, your enjoyment or fulfillment from your experiences is a function of both time and money—in general, the more time and money you spend on experiences, the more fulfillment you'll get from them. But when you're young, healthy, and unjaded, you can get a huge amount of enjoyment even from experiences that don't cost a lot. (Remember my friend Jason, who had the experience of a lifetime while staying in cheap hostels and eating baguettes in the park.) So when you're young and cash poor, my advice is to explore all the free or nearly free experiences you can have. Think of the free outdoor concerts and festivals that city and local governments put on with your tax dollars to make your town wonderful. Or consider how much fun you can have with your friends just talking, hanging out, or playing cards or board games. Or how much of your own town there is to see and explore on foot or by public transportation. Most of us aren't taking anywhere near full advantage of these opportunities for free or virtually free enjoyment. I know I don't—do you?

Choose Your Own Adventure

A lot of experiences are thrust upon you, especially when you're growing up. You have to go to school, and in science class you're told you have to dissect a frog. You might say, "I don't want to dissect this frog." But then your teacher says, "If you don't dissect this frog, you're going to get an F in this course." So you say, "Okay, I'll dissect the frog." You're not given much of a choice there. But when you become an adult, you get to choose many of your experiences: You get to think about how you want to explore life and to decide for yourself where to invest your time and your money, and when to make these investments.

Unfortunately, most people greatly underutilize this freedom. We do make some conscious choices—to some extent, we choose our jobs, our hobbies, our relationships, our vacation destinations. But so much of our life is spent on autopilot—we move through the world as if someone else programmed our actions, and we don't think nearly enough about how to spend our time and money.

This is really easy to see with the coffee habit—such a common example that it's been given a name, "the latte factor." So many people stop every day for a cup of gourmet coffee—and when they do, they barely realize that the cost of all those small indulgences adds up to a lot of money in the course of a year. I'm not here to tell you to skip your daily coffee so you can save up that money to "finish rich"—in fact, the last thing I want for you is to finish rich in money and poor in enjoyable experiences. But imagine all the experiences you could have for the thousands of dollars you are spending on your daily mocha, latte, or Frappuccino.

Of course, when I bring this up, the response I usually get is "I like my daily Starbucks." How can I argue with that? How they feel is how they feel. But what I can and do say is this: "At least be aware of what your Starbucks habit is costing you." For example, you might say to yourself, *I can have a round-trip ticket to anywhere in the United States of America every few months based on what I'm spending on Starbucks. So would I rather have that round-trip ticket or would I rather keep up my coffee habit?* The answer is up to you, and you might choose the lattes, but if you've actively thought through the question and made a deliberate decision, then you're not acting on autopilot.

Making deliberate choices about how to spend your money and your time is the essence of making the most of your life energy.

Recommendations

- Remember that "early" is right now. Of those experiences you thought about earlier, think about which ones would be appropriate to invest in today, this month, or this year. If you're resisting having them now, consider the risk of *not* having them now.
- Think about the people you'd like to have experiences with —and picture the memory dividends you stand to gain from having those experiences sooner rather than later.
- Think about how you can actively enhance your memory dividends. Would it help you to take more photos of your experiences? To plan reunions with people you've shared good times with in the past? Compile a video or a photo album?

3

———

WHY DIE WITH ZERO?

Rule No. 3:
Aim to die with zero.

Staying on autopilot is easy; that's why we use it. But if you're trying to live a full and optimal life, rather than just taking the path of least resistance, autopilot won't give you what you want. To fully enjoy life instead of just surviving it, you need to stop driving mindlessly and actively steer your life the way you want it to go. That won't be the last time I say that—helping you live more deliberately is one of my biggest goals for this book. We need to keep revisiting that theme throughout these pages, because autopilot operates in several areas of your life, from how you earn money to how you give money to other people. Each type of autopilot can create its own form of wasted life energy, and each requires a different strategy for eliminating the waste. This chapter focuses on the type of excess that comes from earning and saving more money than you'll ever get to enjoy. It suggests a deliberate solution for removing that kind of waste.

To show you what I mean, let me tell you about John Arnold, someone I became friends with years before he became a billionaire. After he and I met, he started a hedge fund called Centaurus, with the goal of converting his energy-trading expertise into riches so he could enjoy the good life. But as I worked side by side with him at Centaurus, I could see that, somehow, the good life was constantly getting pushed aside in exchange for making more millions. During one soul-crushing day on the job, John turned to me and said, "Once I make $15 million, if I'm still trading, punch me in the face."

Well, I didn't punch him when he hit that target, and John continued to work as a trader. John is a brilliant guy. (People called him "the king of natural gas" for his unbeatable returns.) John understood perfectly well that at a certain point it makes a lot more sense to spend money doing the things you love than to simply earn more money—but his numerical target kept shifting. He didn't quit when he'd amassed $15 million. He was trading so well that the $15 million became $25 million, which eventually became $100 million, and so on. When you're on a winning streak that big, it's hard to stop, even when your rational mind tells you that you should.

John's life wasn't all work—there were occasional trips to great events, but hardly anything spectacular, like you would imagine for a multimillionaire. In fact, as his wealth grew, his leisure time seemed to diminish. He seemed to think that if he made more money, he could then do more—but in truth, he wasn't doing more.

Still, he kept running Centaurus, and he didn't quit even when he'd reached a net worth of $150 million. In fact, by 2010, the charitable foundation he and his wife had set up had assets of $711 million. He had so much wealth that he was giving millions away. Yet he kept working, even though he didn't exactly love his job. When he did finally quit, in 2012, at age 38, he had built a personal fortune of more than $4 billion.

Now, the vast majority of people can only dream of retiring by the relatively young age of 38—yet for John, that retirement age was actually a few years too late. Why? Two reasons. First, he'll never get those years back that he spent just focusing on making money. He'll never be 30 again, and his children will never again be babies. Second, he made so much money that he now faces the *Brewster's Millions* problem: It's actually hard to spend his fortune fast enough. He already lives in a magnificent house and these days does pretty much what he wants.

One reason he can't use up his money is his kids: Much as he'd enjoy having the über-popular pop band Maroon 5 play private concerts in his backyard every Saturday, for example, he doesn't do anything of the sort, because he doesn't want to spoil his children. He decided to have children, and that decision limits how he can spend his money and his time. Bear in mind that every choice you make affects subsequent choices— and the choice to have children is the most common example of that.

Now, John would say that if he had quit at $15 million, he never would have gotten to $4 billion—an amount that enables him to make a much bigger impact on the social causes he cares about. That's very true. But John would also be the first to admit that he worked past the point of the optimal utility of that money. Did he pass that point at $2 billion? $1.5 billion? Who knows. But we definitely know that it was before he reached $4 billion.

You might also be thinking that John must have been having a wonderful time making all that money if he continued doing it for so long. Maybe he stayed at his trading desk because the thrill of trading was more exciting than anything he could have experienced at home.

But no, John wasn't making a calculated choice between work and family, or between working for money and the millions of other things he could have been doing with his wealth, time, and talent. No, he was continuing to work because he had formed the habit of working, much like a smoker who had picked up cigarettes as a teenage boy because he wanted to look cool to the girls. But now that the boy got the girl, why is he still smoking? Only because he's formed an addictive habit, and habits are hard to break. For some people, it can be the same with working for money—it is just easier to keep doing what you've been doing, especially when what you've been doing continues to reward you with society's universal form of recognition for a job well done, aka money. Once you're in the habit of working for money to live, the thrill of making money exceeds the thrill of *actually living*.

John, of course, is an extreme case, and his situation is the epitome of a high-class problem. But the situation he finds himself in is *not* unique to him, or even just to the ultrarich more generally. So many people feel like they can never get enough, and as their net worth grows, their goalposts just keep shifting. But no matter who you are—a captain of industry or an everyday working stiff—one thing is true: If you spend hours and hours of your life acquiring money and then die without spending all of that money, then you've needlessly wasted too many precious hours of your life. There is just no way to get those hours back. If you die with $1 million left, that's $1 million of experiences you didn't have. And if you die with $50,000 left, well, that's $50,000 of experiences you didn't have. No way is that optimal.

A Waste of Life Energy: Why You Might Be Working for Free

Or look at it another way: Consider all the hours of your life you waste earning money you never spend. Take Elizabeth, a (fictitious) 45-year-old single woman who earns $60,000 a year at her office job in Austin, Texas. This salary puts her in the top half of all 45-year-old income earners in the United States. (All the dollar amounts in this example are in real, inflation-adjusted dollars.) Like most of us, she has to pay income tax, including Social Security and Medicare tax, so her net income is approximately $48,911 per year. She's a hard worker, averaging 50 hours a week, so her net income comes out to $19.56 per hour: That's how much she takes home for every hour she spends at the office.

Thanks to her frugal lifestyle, she was able to pay off her student loans a few years after graduating from college and bought her house when she was in her early thirties, when housing prices in Austin were relatively low. By now, she's paid off the mortgage, so she owns her house outright; if she sold it today, she would get $450,000 for it.

Last year, which was typical, she spent only $32,911 (thus saving exactly $16,000). Elizabeth hopes to retire in 20 years, so she's been putting a good chunk of her paycheck away in a

401(k) and in the bank. She knows the 401(k) plan is an especially good deal, because it uses her pretax dollars, which makes her taxes lower than if she'd put all her money in regular savings accounts. Some employers match employee contributions to the 401(k) plan, but let's say that Elizabeth's does not.

Elizabeth is a reliable worker at a large company, so her job feels secure, and she expects to earn small but steady raises every year until she retires. To keep this example simple, though, let's assume she maintains the same inflation-adjusted salary until she retires. Let's also assume that, besides paying off her house, she didn't start saving for retirement until she was 45. So when she does retire at 65, as planned, she will have saved $320,000 ($16,000 per year for the 20 years between 45 and 65). Therefore, her net worth at 65 will be $770,000 — $320,000 in various retirement accounts and $450,000 in home equity (assuming her house doesn't grow in value).

How long does that $770,000 last her? Well, it depends on how much she spends each year. Research on people's actual retirement spending shows that spending isn't constant, and often declines in later years (as I'll explain shortly). But, again keeping our example simple, let's assume Elizabeth spends exactly $32,000 each year of retirement, or just shy of $1,000 less than she did when she was working. (Again, for the sake of simplicity, let's assume that the return on her retirement investments exactly matches the annual rise in the cost of living.)

With that assumption, her savings will last a little more than 24 years ($770,000 divided by $32,000 per year). But Elizabeth doesn't live another 24 years: She dies at 85, or 20 years after she left the workforce. As a result, she leaves behind $130,000.

I'm telling you this because I want you to really think about the true cost, the terrible waste, of leaving behind $130,000. I've already said that you can think of this money as forgone experiences—whatever the $130,000 could have bought for Elizabeth. That's sad in itself, but it's not only that. By looking at what it took to save that much money—at Elizabeth's hourly rate—you can see how many hours she spent in her office job that she did not need to spend. How many hours was that? Well, divide the $130,000 by $19.56 an hour and you get a little more than 6,646. That's 6,646 hours that Elizabeth worked for money she never got to spend. That's more than two and a half years of 50-hour workweeks! *Two and a half years of working for free.* What a waste of life energy.

The numbers would be even higher if we assumed that her savings earned interest above inflation, and that she would also have income from Social Security. But even under our very conservative assumptions, she would have been better off either retiring earlier or spending more of her money throughout her life.

You might be saying that Elizabeth is not typical. You'd be right, for example, to point out that some people net a much higher hourly rate during their careers. So for those higher earners, $30,000 does not represent as many hours (or years) of unnecessary labor. That is true. But here's the thing: Those people end up dying with much more than $130,000. People who are earning a high hourly rate or a high annual salary are sometimes even more tempted to keep on working and earning. Either way, they are squandering their life energy.

Your own income might be higher or lower than the ones in any of these examples. It doesn't matter, because the conclusion is still the same: If you don't want to squander your life energy, you should aim to spend all your money before you die.

To me, this logic is incontrovertible. Maybe it's because of my training as an engineer, or maybe it's why I chose to study engineering in the first place, but I love efficiency and I hate waste. And I can't think of any worse form of waste than squandering your life energy. So to me it makes perfect sense to want to die with zero. *Not* to reach zero *before* you die, which would leave you high and dry, but to have as little as possible left unused for all the time and energy you spent working to earn that money.

I'm far from the first person to suggest that planning to die with zero is the rational way to live. Back in the 1950s, an economist named Franco Modigliani, who went on to win the Nobel Prize, posited something that came to be known as the Life-Cycle Hypothesis (LCH)—an idea about how people manage their spending and saving to try to get the most from their money *across their life span.* He basically said that making the most of your money in the course of your life requires that, as another economist put it, "wealth will decline to zero by the date of death." In other words, if you know when you will die, you must die with zero—because if you don't, you are not getting maximum enjoyment (utility) from your money. And what about the very real possibility that you don't know when you'll die? Modigliani has a simple answer to that: To be safe but still avoid needlessly leaving money behind, just think of the maximum age to which anyone can live. So a rational person, in Modigliani's view, will spread their wealth across all the years up to the oldest age to which they might live.

Some people do try to live in this rational, utility-maximizing way, but many do not. Either they save too much or they save too little. Optimizing across your whole life takes a lot of thought and planning; it's easier to live for short-term rewards (myopia) and to stay on autopilot (inertia) than to do what will be good for you in the long term. These tendencies can affect both the grasshoppers and the ants among us. Myopia is often the problem of the fun-loving, free-spending grasshopper; inertia can strike the responsible ant as well—particularly later in life, when the dutiful saver must suddenly crack open the nest egg they've so diligently built up. Behavioral economists understand that just because something is rational to do—in this case, switching from saving to "dissaving"—that doesn't mean people will do it easily. Inertia is a very powerful force. As economists Hersh Shefrin and Richard Thaler once put it, "It is hard to teach an old household new rules."

Dying with zero strikes me as such a clear and important goal that I want to go right to the next step: helping you figure out how to actually achieve that goal. But I've discussed these ideas with enough people to know that I can't jump straight to the how: The same small set of questions and objections come up again and again, and I know I can't ignore them. So I will first respond to these common "whatabouts"—and if you're still with me about the value and feasibility of dying with zero, we'll move on to some tools that can help you make that happen.

"But I Love My Job!"

When I say that leaving money behind amounts to a waste of life energy or to working for free, I sometimes hear from people who say that my analysis doesn't apply to them because they love their jobs. Some people go so far as to say that they would *pay* to pursue the work they love—something I doubted until I began dating a professional dancer. (Not the stripper kind!) Dance is an extremely competitive field, with many more people auditioning than there are paying gigs to go around—and, unlike in acting or some other competitive fields, you can never get wealthy dancing, no matter how successful you become.

Nonetheless, just to stay in the game, you have to constantly take dance lessons to stay proficient and you have to live near one of the centers of the dance world, expensive cities like New York and Los Angeles. So most dancers have to take on other jobs that, in effect, subsidize their passion for dance. So, yes, I get that some people love their work and see it as a fulfilling life experience in its own right. And I think that's wonderful—we should all be so lucky!

But, all that being said, I still think they would be better off dying with zero, and here's why. First, let's look at their side of the argument, which goes something like this: If your job itself is a fun, fulfilling experience, then any money you earn from doing the work is just a by-product—like the pile of ash left after a wood fire. When you lit the fire, creating ash wasn't your goal; you enjoyed the fire's warmth and flickering light, and you just happened to get some ash from the process, too. No harm there, and certainly no harm in making money from pursuing the work you love.

But here's the thing: Even people who see work as a form of play would be better off if they spent at least some percentage of their time on experiences that *don't* involve working for money. Even if dance is your life, chances are you won't enjoy doing it 24/7. Also, when you're in your forties, fifties, or sixties, you might want to spend a lower percentage of your week dancing than when you were in your twenties and thirties.

Of course, it's possible that you won't want to cut back your hours as you get older—you might really want to keep dancing (or practicing law or psychotherapy or whatever profession you enjoy) full-time as long as you're able, and earning money doing it. Be my guest! Just be sure to spend the money that you earn on whatever you value: Take more first-class trips, throw better parties, go to see your favorite dancer perform live. Because even if you enjoyed every minute of the work that brought you that money, failing to spend that money is still a waste. To use a metaphor from video games, it's as if you earned an extra life and then decided to throw that extra life away—you just let Mario jump off a bridge instead of taking the little guy further through the Mushroom Kingdom. Would you do that only because you weren't counting on that extra life? Why take that easy-come, easy-go attitude? It's the same with any money you receive. "Maximizing your life" *doesn't care where the money came from.* Whether you earn it from a job you love or you inherit it from your great-granddad, whether the money is a by-product of following your passion or of being a member of the lucky-sperm club, once it's given to you it becomes yours. And once it's yours, it now represents hours of *your* life, which you can exchange for whatever will help you live the best life you can. If dance is your life, and you happen to also earn money from dancing, go ahead and spend it on dance-related experiences: Splurge on private lessons with the best dance teachers if that's what you value, or hire someone to clean your place so you have more time to pursue dance. Just don't let that money sit and go to waste because of where it came from. The source of your money doesn't change the calculus on maximizing your life.

"But . . . But . . ."

When I say the words "die with zero," most people's immediate reaction is fear, quickly followed by the thought that dying with money left isn't a total waste, because that money will go to your heirs, or maybe to charity. The most common expression of this belief is "What about the kids?"

The kids question comes up so often, and there is so much to say about it, that it deserves its own chapter—and indeed it gets one, along with my thoughts on charitable giving. But for now, let me just touch on my answer to the kids question.

First of all, yes, you can certainly leave money to the people and causes you care about—but the truth is that those people and causes would be better off getting your wealth sooner rather than later. Why wait until after you die?

Second, whatever amount you give to others immediately becomes their money, not yours. But when I talk about dying with zero, I am talking about *your* money. Whatever you've given your kids will remain theirs, so there is no need to plan to have money left over for them. You'll learn much more about how to deliberately plan what to leave, to whom, and when in a later chapter, "What About the Kids?"

Now let me address the fear. Many people have told me they're scared—even terrified—that they'll run out of money before they die. And I get it. Nobody wants to spend their last years in poverty, so it's understandable that people save for the future. And I'm not saying you *shouldn't* save for the future. What I'm saying is that people who save tend to save *too* much for *too late* in their lives. They are depriving themselves now just to care for a much, much older future self—a future self that may never live long enough to enjoy that money.

People Who Save Too Much

How do I know that people save too much for too late? I've seen the statistics. If you look at data on net worth by age, you find that most people keep accumulating wealth for decades, and most don't start spending it down until very late in life.

The Federal Reserve Board tracks how much Americans have built up at various stages of their lives. For example, we know from its most recent Survey of Consumer Finances that the median net worth for U.S. households headed by someone aged 45 to 54 is $124,200. That just means that half of households in this age group have saved up at least $124,200, while half have saved up less than that—some of them have saved much more, and others have saved much less. What's much more interesting than the median for this one age range is the overall trend. By look-

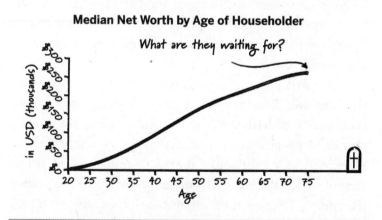

Americans' median net worth keeps rising at least until their mid-seventies.

ing at the net-worth numbers for other ages, you can see a clear pattern: The median net worth continues to rise as people get older.

It's easy to guess why—people's annual incomes tend to rise with age, and people continue to save what they don't spend, so their nest egg keeps growing. And that's great to a point, because there is a sweet spot in everyone's lifetime during which they can most enjoy the fruits of their wealth. The problem is that people continue to save well past that optimal point. So American heads of household between the ages of 65 and 74 have a median net worth of $224,100, up from the $187,300 saved up by householders between 55 and 64. That's crazy—people in their seventies are still saving for the future! In fact, even in their mid-seventies, people in this upper half of the population don't start dipping into their savings. The median net worth for American householders aged 75 or older is the highest of all the age groups: $264,800. So even with rising life expectancies, millions of Americans are on track to have their hard-earned money outlive them. Yes, older people often save in anticipation of healthcare costs—but, as you'll see shortly, people's overall expenses decline with age, even counting the cost of healthcare.

Other data points in the same direction. A 2018 study from the Employee Benefit Research Institute used data on older Americans' wealth (income and assets) and their spending to see how much people's assets changed during their first 20 years of retirement. ("Or until death," the study's authors added, as if to remind readers that not everyone gets to enjoy a full 20 years of retirement.) In other words, were people spending down their assets, or were they largely preserving them? Here are some of their key findings:

- On the whole, people are very slow to spend down ("decumulate") their assets.

- Across ages, whether looking at retirees in their sixties or those in their nineties, the median ratio of household spending to household income hovers around 1:1. This means that people's spending continues to closely track their income—so as people's incomes decline, their spending does, too. This is another way of seeing that retirees aren't really drawing down all the money they've saved up.

- At the high end, retirees who had $500,000 or more right before retirement had spent down a median of only 11.8 percent of that money 20 years later or by the time they died. That's more than 88 percent left over—which means that a person retiring at 65 with half a million dollars still has more than $440,000 left at age 85!

- At the lower end, retirees with less than $200,000 saved up for retirement spent a higher percentage (as you might expect, since they had less to spend overall)—but even this group's median members had spent down only one-quarter of their assets 18 years after retirement.

- One-third of all retirees actually *increased* their assets after retirement! Instead of slowly or quickly decumulating, they continued to accumulate wealth.

- Retirees on a pension—meaning that they had a guaranteed source of ongoing income after retirement—spent down much less of their assets (only 4 percent) during the first 18 years after retirement than did non-pensioners (who had spent down 34 percent).

So, clearly, people who, back in their working years, would have said they were saving up for retirement are not actually spending those retirement savings once they reach retirement. They are definitely *not* on track to die with zero. Some of them appear to not even *aim* to die with zero; this is especially clear when you look at people with pensions. Pensioners could dip more deeply into their savings than anyone, since their guaranteed income for life assures them they will never starve. But, interestingly, pensioners spend down the lowest percentage of their wealth, probably because, as the data shows, that they had more wealth to begin with.

So the question remains: Why didn't retirees spend more of their money when they were young enough to enjoy it more fully? What were they waiting for?!

There are a couple of answers to that question. The first is that people did have good intentions to spend the money, but once they reached a certain age, they found that their wants and needs changed, or perhaps diminished. Experts in retirement planning even have some lingo for this consumption pattern: go-go years, slow-go years, and no-go years. The idea is that when you're first retired, you're raring to have all those experiences you've been putting off until retirement, and you still (for the most part) have the health and energy to pursue those experiences. Those are your go-go years. Later on, typically in your seventies, you begin to slow down as you cross items off your bucket list and your health declines. And later still, in your eighties or beyond, you don't have a whole lot of "go" left at all, no matter how much money you still have. As one retirement-planning adviser put it, "My dad is 86 and he doesn't want to go anywhere, just stay close to home."

I saw something like this firsthand with my grandma when she was in her late seventies and I was in my late twenties. I was just starting to make it as a trader and was excited to share my new wealth with the people I love, and my grandma was one of those people. So I gave her a $10,000 check. It feels like a dumb gift now, and if I knew then what I know now, I would have given her an actual memorable experience instead, such as a trip to visit relatives in another state. But back then, I was of the mind that people know best what to give themselves. I would have wanted someone to just give me the money, so that's exactly what I did for my grandma.

My grandma was living with my mom in those days, so once in a while I'd ask my mom what Grandma had spent the money on. And it turned out that Grandma wasn't spending it at all. It's not that she was poor and needed it to pay the bills. She just didn't have a lot of "go" left. When Christmas rolled around that year, Grandma presented me with a gift: a sweater. To this day, as far as I know, that sweater (which I would guess cost about $50) was the only thing that ever came of my $10,000 gift. There was no incremental joy she got from that transfer of $10,000, aside from whatever joy she got from getting me that sweater, or from knowing that her grandson wanted to give her money.

But for whatever reason, she just could not spend the money. She was just too thrifty for her own good—someone who actually kept every couch, love seat, and easy chair covered in plastic to protect the upholstery from wear and tear. Unfortunately, of course, the plastic also made the furniture uncomfortable and unattractive. One day I came into my grandmother's house for somebody's funeral and sat on a colorful, comfy couch—she had taken the plastic off for this special occasion. But the next time I visited, all the plastic was back on, and it stayed on for the rest of my grandmother's life. This never made sense to me: Why spend all this money on furniture that you don't get to enjoy? The plastic over the couches is a microcosmic example of much of what I'm talking about in this book: the senselessness of indefinitely delayed gratification.

You might think that as people get older, they spend money more freely out of the sheer desire to make the most of it before it's truly too late. But the opposite tends to happen. In general, spending among American households declines as people age. For example, the Consumer Expenditure Survey, conducted by the Bureau of Labor Statistics, found that in 2017, average annual spending for households headed by 55-to-64-year-olds was $65,000; average spending fell to $55,000 for those between 65 and 74; and spending fell again to $42,000 for those 75 and older. This overall decline occurred *despite* a rise in healthcare expenses, because most other expenses, such as clothing and entertainment, were much lower. The decline in spending over time was even more acute for retirees with more than $1 million in assets, according to separate research conducted by J.P. Morgan Asset Management, which analyzed data from more than half a million of its customers.

Many financial planners are very familiar with this pattern. On sites that provide retirement advice, references to the "slow-go" and "no-go" years abound. But the message of declining "go" doesn't seem to have reached the general public. And if you're not aware of this fairly predictable pattern, you're likely to (incorrectly) expect steady expenditures on experiences from the day you retire until the day you die. That's one reason you might greatly oversave and underspend.

An Abundance of Caution

But there's another, more intentional reason why people routinely save too much and spend too little, leaving money behind for when they die. Some people never actually planned to spend all that money on life experiences but instead were saving for the unforeseen expenses of old age, especially medical expenses. It's not just that everyone's health declines as they get on in years, creating higher medical expenses toward the end of their lives. It's also that the actual expenses are hard to predict: Will you need triple bypass surgery or years' worth of treatment for cancer? Will you have to spend years in a nursing home?

In theory, that's what insurance is for: to protect against whatever calamity might strike. But even people with insurance sometimes find themselves with high medical bills. This can happen because of high deductibles or costly prescription co-pays, or just because the insurer for some reason denies coverage. Since most people want to stay alive after falling ill, it's natural and reasonable to save up for medical care. And when the costs of care are uncertain, people tend to save even more.

Yet even after taking the uncertainty of costs into account, many people *still* save too much. To me, that's like going out and buying something silly, like alien robot invasion insurance. That is, assuming there's some very, very tiny possibility that alien robots could invade our planet and wreak havoc on our lives, does that mean you should build a special shelter to protect yourself? I'd rather take my chances and use the money for something more useful and more enjoyable.

Planning for your medical care by saving money is a lot like that, even though it is true that you're much more likely to need costly medical care than to see heavily armed and ultra-intelligent extraterrestrials. To put it bluntly, no amount of savings available to most people will cover the costliest healthcare you might possibly need. For example, cancer treatments can easily cost half a million dollars a year.

Or, if your out-of-pocket medical expenses amount to $50,000 per *night* (as they did for my father's hospital stay at the end of his life), does it really matter whether you've saved $10,000 or $50,000 or even $250,000? No, it doesn't, because the extra $50,000 will buy you *one* extra night, a night that might well have taken you a year's worth of work to earn! Similarly, $250,000 saved over however many years will get wiped out in five days. I'm not suggesting that you should rack up large hospital costs with a plan to then stiff the hospital on those bills. What I'm saying is that you can't pay your way out of high-priced end-of-life medical care; since uninsured medical care is so expensive, it won't make any real difference for the vast majority of us whether we save for it or not. Either the government will pay for it or you will die.

But let's say you're not part of the vast majority—let's say you're worth millions or tens of millions. What then? Even if I earn enough that I *could* save up for a few extra months of life in the hospital, I can't see the logic in doing that: There's a big difference between living a life and just being kept alive, and I'd much rather spend on the former. So I will not work for years to save up for a few more months on a ventilator with a quality of life that's close to zero—or, depending on the level of suffering, maybe even negative. So instead of engaging in "precautionary saving," as economists call the practice, I'll let the cards fall where they may. We all die sooner or later, and I'd rather die when the time is right than sacrifice my better years just to squeeze out a few more days at the tail end. Or, as I like to say, "See you at the grave!"

Besides, it is much smarter to spend your healthcare money on the front end (to maintain your health and try to prevent disease) than to spend it at the end, when you get a lot less bang for every buck you spend. In fact, many insurance companies not only cover preventive care such as mammograms but believe enough in the long-term cost savings of disease prevention that they actually pay you (in the form of gift cards, for example) to get regular screenings and other preventive care. You won't be able to avert every possible illness, no matter what you do, but you can make some health problems a lot less likely—and you'll enjoy better quality of life all along the way.

It might sound like I'm urging you to focus all your efforts on your youth and to not give a second thought to what happens when you're old and frail. But that would be a misleading distortion of what I'm saying. Even though it's a huge mistake to greatly sacrifice your quality of life now for better quality of life in old age, I do understand the desire to be taken care of when you're old and vulnerable. So how do you make sure you're covered if you need long-term care, without having to save up massive amounts of money you won't spend if you don't need nursing care? The answer: long-term care insurance. Look into it and you might discover that it costs less than you think, especially if you start paying premiums before you're 65.

There's a more general point I want to get across: For every single thing you might be worried about in your future, there is an insurance product to protect you. That doesn't mean I recommend buying insurance for every single thing; obviously, insurance costs money. But the fact that insurance companies are willing to sell insurance for various risks shows that these risks can be quantified—and removed for those who don't want to take those risks.

In this chapter, I've tried to show you *why* dying with zero is a worthy goal—a way to prevent one major waste of life energy. But what about the *how*? If you're like most people, you're still doubtful about the feasibility of actually hitting this goal, especially given the uncertainty about how long you will live. The *how* is the subject of the next chapter.

Recommendations

- If you're still concerned and resisting the idea of dying with zero, try to figure out where this psychological resistance comes from.
- If you love your job, and you love going to work every day, identify ways that you can spend your money on activities that fit your work schedule.

4

HOW TO SPEND YOUR MONEY (WITHOUT ACTUALLY HITTING ZERO BEFORE YOU DIE)

Rule No. 4:
Use all available tools to
help you die with zero.

If you're still with me, I assume you agree that trying to die with zero is a good idea, at least in principle. But you are probably skeptical about the feasibility of hitting this goal.

And you are right to be skeptical. In fact, dying with *exactly* zero is an impossible goal. To attain it would require knowing exactly when you're going to die—but none of us is God, so we can't know the day we're going to die.

Still, just because we can't predict the *exact* date doesn't mean we can't get close. Let me explain. Have you ever used a life expectancy calculator? Many insurance companies offer them for free on their Web sites, and I think they're kind of fun to try out. These calculators are, admittedly, imprecise tools, but in order to forecast how long you'll live, they ask a series of questions about your current age, your gender, height, and weight (how good is your BMI?), smoking and drinking patterns, and other major predictors of overall health. Some also ask about your family history and whether you use a seat belt. After you've answered all the questions, the calculator typically gives you a number—you'll live to be 94! (Or 55 if you don't lose 90 pounds and quit drinking like a sailor and smoking a pack a day.)

Trying to figure out how long you'll live might not be your idea of fun; it might feel like a morbid exercise, right up there with planning your funeral and listing your beneficiaries on a life insurance form. Fine. You don't have to love it for it to be worth doing. If you don't want to use a life expectancy calculator, that's your choice—just don't tell me you have no idea how long you'll live, and then use that as an excuse to save money like you're going to live to be 150.

Whatever number the calculator comes up with is just an estimate derived by actuaries, the experts hired by insurers to forecast risk based on relevant statistics. If the calculator gives you one number, you can think of it as just an educated guess based on the past life spans of people who are roughly like you. Many people who are like you died younger than this average, and many died older. So there's an average and there's also a range. To reflect this reality, some life expectancy calculators report their results in probabilities. They might tell you, for example, that you have a 50 percent chance of living to 92, a 10 percent chance of living to 100, and so on. These probabilities just go to show that predicting life expectancy for one individual is an inexact science. But knowing only the probabilities of survival to a given age is still better than not knowing at all. If you don't have any idea when you'll die, you won't be able to make decisions that are anywhere close to optimal. That means that if you're the cautious type, you'll just save and spend as if you expect to live to be 150; you might even act as if you expect to live forever, like those people who never dip into their principal and live only on the interest earned. As a result, you will die with much, much more than zero—which means you will have wasted many hours of your life energy earning money that you will never get to enjoy.

Knowing at least approximately when you're going to die will help you make much better decisions about earning, saving, and spending. So I urge you: Go ahead and try a life expectancy calculator.

You might be wondering which particular calculator to use. I posed this question to the Society of Actuaries, since they're the real experts. They wouldn't endorse a certain calculator but instead referred me to their own Web site (soa.org), which mainly provides tools for professional actuaries. There is one very accessible tool their Web site recommends: the Actuaries Longevity Illustrator (http://www.longevityillustrator.org/). Based on your answers to just a few questions, it produces a chart that shows your probabilities of dying at different ages. Its point is to show you the risk of outliving your resources—but by looking at the extreme, you can see how low a probability there is that you will live past a certain age.

Another approach is to ask your insurance agent, and many insurance companies that sell life insurance offer free online calculators for anyone to use.

If you'd like to get a more precise estimate of your life expectancy based on additional health factors, you'll need to answer more health and lifestyle questions. One helpful tool is the Living to 100 calculator (https://www.livingto100.com), designed by a doctor and researcher who studies exceptional longevity.

What did you discover after trying one or more of these tools? If you tried multiple calculators, how consistent were the results? Are you likely to die later than you'd thought? Are you thinking you might want to change your lifestyle, or see what happens if you rerun the calculation in a few years? All good questions, and thinking about them is a first step toward optimizing your spending.

But how? Given that we want to die with zero, and given that hitting exactly zero is impossible, how do you get close to zero? How do you deal with the variance of human life?

The first item to confront is the uncertainty. The possibility that you will live longer than you expect is called *longevity risk*. Nobody wants to die early—the possibility of that is called *mortality risk*—but nobody wants to die after their money runs out either. (With no money, your quality of life will take a dramatic dip, to put it mildly.) So there's uncertainty on both sides of our expected life span, and we want to figure out how to deal with the negative financial consequences of that uncertainty.

For that, as noted, there are financial products. Now, I don't really want to be pushing financial products, and I definitely don't want to get into their minutiae (which I am no expert on), but there are some basic elements you really need to understand before you decide that dying with zero is not for you. And I don't have to be a certified financial adviser to tell you what those basic elements are—any more than I need to be an auto mechanic to tell you that if you want to drive yourself across the country you'll need a car.

You Are Not a Good Insurance Agent!

You probably already know about the financial product used to deal with mortality risk, the risk of dying early. That's life insurance, of course. Life insurance companies don't know exactly when you'll die, just as you don't — but they can nonetheless pay your beneficiaries when you die, whenever that happens to be. The insurers can do that with great certainty, because they are simultaneously insuring millions of other people: Some of these insured will die earlier than average, but others will die later, so the "errors" on both sides will cancel each other out. That means an insurance company doesn't need to know when you yourself will die — they just need to know enough life expectancy data about their total insurance pool to make sure they can pay out and still make a profit overall.

This ability to pool risk across a large number of people is what gives insurance companies their edge over you as an individual. It's why people are willing to pay money to buy insurance of all kinds, instead of trying to protect themselves from risk on their own. *You are not a good insurance agent.*

So that's life insurance — it helps you deal with mortality risk, and 60 percent of Americans own at least some life insurance. What fewer people realize is that there are financial products designed to deal with longevity risk, too. Since many people are fearful of running out of money before they pass on, there is one product that they should definitely look into. These products are called *income annuities* (or simply *annuities*). Annuities are essentially the opposite of life insurance: When you buy life insurance, you're spending money to protect your survivors against the risk that you'll die too young, whereas buying annuities protects you against the risk of dying too old (outliving your savings).

If you don't want to hear it from me, listen to Ron Lieber, *The New York Times'* "Your Money" columnist. "The insurance companies that create annuities often make them seem like investments," he wrote in a recent explainer about annuities. "But really they're more like insurance." Lieber went on: "Like insurance to stave off financial disaster, an annuity is something you purchase to guarantee that you won't run out of money if you live a long time."

In fact, thinking of annuities as insurance makes them a lot more sensible than thinking of them as investments—because as investments they are not good at all. But that's not their goal —their goal is to insure you against the risk of outliving your money.

How do they achieve that goal? Well, buying an annuity means you give the insurance company a lump sum—say, $500,000 at age 60—and in return you get a guaranteed monthly payout (for example, $2,400 each month) for the rest of your life, however long that happens to be. Like all insurance, annuities aren't free—insurance companies have to make money to stay in business!—but if your goal is to maximize the life experiences you can buy with the money you've earned, they're a very sensible solution. That's partly because, even after the insurance company's fees, your monthly payouts amount to more than you would probably be willing to pay yourself if you wanted to make sure you didn't outlive your money. For example, one popular rule of thumb for retirement spending is the "4 percent rule," whereby you withdraw 4 percent from your savings each year of retirement. Well, with annuities, your annual payouts will probably amount to more than 4 percent of what you put into the annuity—and, unlike the 4 percent withdrawals, those payouts are guaranteed to continue for the rest of your life.

The reason the insurance company can give you a rate of return that is both steady and reasonably high is that you are not leaving any money on the table. You relinquish your principal forever. In the extreme case—if you die the day after you buy the annuity—you won't see any more of the money you put in, and it will instead go to monthly payments to the lucky stranger (another annuity buyer) who lives into her nineties. Without an annuity, on the other hand, you are forced to self-insure—to be your own insurance agent. That's not a great idea, because unlike the insurance agents who work for big insurance companies, you don't have the ability to pool risk and cancel out errors on both sides. So, to feel financially secure until the end of your days, you will have to leave a large cushion to cover the worst-case scenario: You will have to oversave, which means that more likely than not you will end up dying with considerable money left over. You'll have worked for years earning money that you never got to enjoy. So by trying to play insurance agent, you are not even close to maximizing your life. Again, this is why you are not a good insurance agent!

Economists generally think that annuities are such a rational way to deal with longevity risk that many experts have long wondered why more people don't buy annuities—a question economists call "the annuity puzzle."

So am I telling you to go plunk down all your savings in an annuity? No, of course not. But what I am saying is that there exist solutions to the problem of how to die with zero without running out of money, and you'd be doing yourself a disservice if you didn't at least look into them.

Again, remember that the goal is to eliminate as much waste as possible. How close you get to that goal depends on your own risk tolerance. If you have a very low tolerance for risk—meaning you will not accept even a tiny chance of outliving your money—you will either buy an annuity or you will self-insure by leaving a huge cushion. The odds that you will live to be 123 are currently very low. (The oldest person on record died when she was 122 years and 164 days.) But if you are extremely risk averse, then you will leave a cushion big enough to last you through your 123rd year.

On the flip side, if you are comfortable living on the edge, you don't need this book, because you are probably already on track to die with zero. Well, not really—you still need this book, because when you live perilously close to the edge, you risk outliving your money. In general, though, the higher your tolerance for longevity risk, the less of a cushion you will need. So the more risk you are willing to take, the less of your life energy you're likely to waste working for money you won't ever get to spend.

For example, suppose your life expectancy is 85, but you want to allow for an error of 5 to 6 percent. If so, you might decide to save for a few extra years—in this case, enough to last you until you're 90. But if you don't want to have wasted five years' worth of savings in case you do die as expected at 85, you can eliminate that waste (and live a little better between now and then) by saving a little less—as long as you're okay with the risk.

I am not telling you which way is right: Risk tolerance is a singular and personal preference. But I do want you to know that there is a big difference between thinking about your risk tolerance and acting out of blind fear. So it's fine to look at your life expectancy, to consider your risk tolerance, and to do the math to figure out how many years you need to save for. But that's not the same as being so frightened of outliving your money —or of the thought of death—that you avoid even looking at the numbers. If you live your life with fear and avoidance, my bet is you will either fritter your money away or play it so safe that you will leave many, many years of your hard-earned money behind—so you'll be working many years as a slave to your own fears.

What Problem Are You Solving?

A caution: Annuities can be very complicated—entire books have been written about them. For starters, there are several different types. Also, depending on a whole host of factors—such as your age and health, your total savings, and your tolerance for risk—you might be better off bypassing annuities completely or using a mix of retirement investments, of which annuities are just one.

Financial advisers can help you sort these things out—I don't blame you for not wanting to read a book about annuities! But you can't be totally ignorant. And you have to be clear about what you want the adviser to do. First you need to understand that some financial advisers don't particularly want to bring up annuities: If your adviser gets paid a percentage of what financial professionals call your "assets under management," their incentive is to accumulate assets under management. The last thing they want is for you to take all your money out of the portfolio they are managing for you. After all, for them, annuities are the competition.

But let's assume you are working with a fee-only adviser, someone you pay a flat fee for giving you financial advice. This kind of adviser doesn't have an incentive to avoid annuities and also doesn't get paid commissions for selling annuities. Great —no conflicts of interest in either direction. Your adviser can do the mental gymnastics to come up with a plan for you. But you first have to tell them clearly what your goal is, what problem you are trying to solve. If you've got a roofing problem, don't call the plumber. The best plumber in the world won't fix your leaky roof. Likewise, your financial adviser might be a great stock picker, but that's helpful only if the problem they are solving is for you to be as rich as possible—whereas we're solving for your total life enjoyment.

Let me say that again: *We are solving for your total life enjoyment.*

That is, the premise of this book is that you should be focusing on maximizing your life enjoyment rather than on maximizing your wealth. Those are two very different goals. Money is just a means to an end: Having money helps you to achieve the more important goal of enjoying your life. But trying to maximize money actually gets in the way of achieving the more important goal.

So always keep this end goal in mind. Make "maximize total life enjoyment" your mantra, using it to guide every decision— including what to focus on with your financial adviser. If you tell your fee-only financial adviser that you are trying to get as much enjoyment out of your savings as possible without outliving your savings, they can help you create a plan for making that happen.

The part of that plan that I've been focusing on in this chapter is how to avoid running out of money—how not to outspend your savings. But of course that's just one half of the question of how to die with zero; the other half is how not to waste your life energy by underspending. So what's the plan for spending down your money so you don't die with leftover assets and a pile of regrets? In the language of financial advisers, how should you plan to "decumulate" the money you've been accumulating over the years? My full answer to that question comes in chapter 8, "Know Your Peak," but let me just give you a brief preview here. It starts with tracking your health so you know when to start spending more than you are earning (when to crack open your nest egg). It also means knowing your projected death date and your *annual cost of just staying alive,* because those two numbers together tell you the bare minimum amount you will need between now and the end of your life.

All your savings beyond that amount is money you must aggressively spend down on experiences that you enjoy. I say "aggressively" because your declining health and diminishing interests mean that your list of activities will narrow as you age, which means that your spending rate won't remain constant: If you want to die with zero and make the most of whatever health you have at every point in your lifetime, you will need to spend more in your fifties than in your sixties, and more in your sixties than in your seventies, let alone your eighties and nineties! Chapter 8 further explains these ideas and gives you tools for implementing them, by yourself or with the help of a financial adviser.

Final Countdown

Like all living creatures, humans have evolved to survive. Of course, we want to do more than just survive; for example, I'm sure if I asked you if you want to survive or really thrive, you'd choose thriving. But our biology is such that efforts to live the best life we can often don't come as naturally or as strongly as the basic instinct to survive. Avoiding death is our number one priority, and that single goal dwarfs everything else. My friend Cooper Richey put it well when he said, "The human brain is wired to be irrational about death." People avoid the subject of death, they behave as if it's never coming, and too many don't plan for it. It's just some sort of mystery date in one's future when we expire.

This kind of blanket denial explains why so many people are willing to spend tens or even hundreds of thousands of dollars to prolong life for just a few more weeks. Think about it: That's money that they spent years or decades working hard for. They gave up *years* of their life *while healthy and vibrant* to buy a few extra *weeks* of life when they are *sick and immobile.* If that's not irrational, I don't know what is!

Granted, money has absolutely no value to you when you're dead—that's why I say you should die with zero. Because of that, it's not irrational once you're near the end to spend all of your remaining money to prolong life even a little bit. At that point, it's use-it-or-lose-it. As a trio of high-powered economists have written, "A substantial amount of spending on futile care is rational when there is no value of leaving wealth behind."

But that statement is true only if you failed to plan and are therefore now finding yourself trying to make the best of a bad situation. And why would you get into this bad situation? Not on purpose, that's for sure. You would never get to that point if you thought rationally *ahead of time* and made plans when your health was good—because a *plan* to spend a huge portion of your wealth during the last few weeks of life makes no sense. It's totally irrational.

But here's the problem: People are irrational about death even when they are not close to death. That's why they have out-size fears of running out of money before they die—big enough to compel many people to oversave for the distant future and, as a result, fail to enjoy their present as much as they could.

But death and deterioration are real for everyone, so the date of your death in the future *should* affect what your behavior is now. Think of it one step at a time, starting with the most extreme case: If you knew that you were going to die tomorrow, your behavior and activities today would obviously change, maybe even taking a 180-degree turn. Now take it down just a notch: If you were two days away from death, your behavior and activities would change a little differently, but they'd still be dramatically different than if you had 50 or 75 more years to live. Now think about how your behavior would change if you knew you had three days until your death. What if you had 365 days? Now imagine iterating through this loop until you get to 14,000 days or 25,000 days or whatever actual number of days you probably have. Note how this line of thinking extends to your actual death date and changes your plans.

Also notice that I'm *not* saying you should live today as if it's your last day. We always have to balance living in the present with planning for the future, and the balance tilts gradually as you shift your death date out: The closer your death date is, the more urgency you need to have, and the further away it is, the more you can and should plan for the future. But if we fail to look at our death date at all, we act as if we will live forever —and then there's no way are we going to get the balance anywhere close to right.

At the same time, thinking about death can be distressing, so we tend to avoid thinking about it, and we behave as if it is never going to happen. We keep putting off wonderful experiences, as if in our final month we can easily squeeze in all those experiences that we had put off all our lives. Needless to say, that's not possible—so it's totally irrational.

I know it may sound morbid and it might make you uncomfortable, but I've actually started using an app called Final Countdown that counts down the days (and years, months, weeks, and so on) before my estimated death date, and I have been urging all my friends to do the same. Yes, I can see how this app could be unnerving, but the reminder of death gives a much-needed urgency to one's life.

By seeing how many weeks I've got left, for example, I'm reminded how many (or how few) weekends I've got. Seeing the number of years reminds me that I've got only so many Christmases to enjoy, or so many summers or autumns. And those in-your-face reminders have changed my thoughts and the things I do—like the people I reach out to, and how often I tell people I love them. Final Countdown makes me a better match against the autopilot instincts that would have me act as if death didn't exist. Death, of course, does exist. In fact, as I explain in a later chapter, we all die a thousand deaths before our one final death.

And Final Countdown is one tool that can help us live a life more mindful of that reality.

What I'm saying is that dying with zero is not only about money: It's also about time. Start thinking more about how you use your limited time, your life energy, and you'll be well on your way to living the fullest life you possibly can.

Recommendation

If you're nervous about someday running out of money before you die, then spend some time looking to annuities as a possible solution.

5

WHAT ABOUT THE KIDS?

Rule No. 5:
Give money to your children or to
charity when it has the most impact.

Every single time I talk about dying with zero, I get some version
of the same question: What about the kids? This question always
comes up, without fail, no matter who I talk to.

A couple of variations of this question even have a moraliz-
ing, self-sacrificial tone. Some people have actually said to me,
"Well, that's what somebody would say who doesn't have kids."
And even when they know I have children—two daughters—
some people will still imply that dying with zero is the ultimate
act of selfishness. No matter how they put it, what most people
who ask about the kids mean is this: Planning to die with zero

might be good for someone thinking only about themselves, but shouldn't you care about the well-being of your children, too? Because if you cared about someone other than yourself, you wouldn't die with zero. You would make sure to leave money for the kids. Their implication: If dying with zero is a philosophy only for selfish bastards, then it can't possibly be the right philosophy for decent, caring people like themselves.

That's the holier-than-thou attitude I hear from so many people, and I have no patience for it, because it's so hypocritical. Too often, people who make comments about the kids to argue against the Die with Zero way aren't actually putting their children first but instead are treating their kids as an afterthought. Why do I say that? Well, let me give you an example from a typical conversation with my closest friends.

When one of these good friends poses this inevitable question—"What about the kids?"—I first explain that the money you're leaving to your kids is *not* your money. So when I say you should die with zero, I'm not saying: Die with zero and spend all your kids' money along the way. I'm saying: Spend all *your* money.

That is, give your children whatever you have allocated for them before you die. Why wait until you're gone?

Remember, these are conversations I'm having with my closest friends, and we always call each other out on our BS. So I tell them straight out, "You're full of BS! Where's your trust fund for your kids? How much is it set to? When is it going to distribute? *Have you even thought about these things, or are you just parroting what you've heard?*"

Do you see what I'm saying? If you're really putting your kids first, as you claim you are, don't wait until you're dead to show your generosity. (I like to say that dead people can't give money away—they can't do anything.) Putting your kids first means you give to them *much earlier,* and you make a deliberate plan to make sure that what you have for your children reaches them when it will make the most impact. A real plan for dying with zero includes the kids, if you have kids. That way, you've already separated out their money (which becomes untouchable by you) from your money, which is what you must spend down to zero. That's my short answer to the question about the kids. The rest of this chapter provides the full version.

Dying to Give the Money Away: The Problem with Inheritances

When people bring up the kids, they're saying that anyone planning to die with zero won't leave a bequest—the kids won't get an inheritance, and what a terrible outcome for the children that is. The crazy thing is that these are often the same people who say you should save as much as you can for your retirement because you don't know when you'll die. Well, if you don't know when you'll die, and you care so much about your kids, why do you want to wait until that random date for your offspring to get what you want them to have? In fact, what makes you so sure that all of your kids will even be alive by the time you die?

This is the problem with inheritances: You're leaving too much to chance. Remember, life can be extremely fickle. Regardless of the amount you're passing on, it takes a great deal of luck for it to arrive exactly when each of your recipients needs the money most. Much more likely, the money will arrive too late for it to have maximum impact on the recipient's quality of life.

What would you guess is the most common age for people to get an inheritance? Well, people at the Federal Reserve Board track such things, and here's what they find: For any income group you look at, the age of "inheritance receipt" peaks at around 60. In other words, if you were betting on how old someone will be when they inherit money—assuming you know nothing else except that they stand to inherit—60 is your best bet. (That's a natural result of the fact that the most common life span is 80 and the most common age gap between parents and children is 20, the report points out.)

Of course, there's a spread around that peak of age 60—many people who get an inheritance get it earlier than that, and many get it later. Overall, the data falls into more or less a normal (bell-shaped) distribution. So for every 100 people who inherit at around age 40 (which is 20 years before the age of peak inheritances), there are 100 people who inherit around age 80! It's true that some people may be getting inheritances from people other than their parents—the older the recipients are, the more likely that is to be the case. But it doesn't matter—whether people are getting inheritances from their parents or from someone else, the data clearly shows many people getting inheritances late in life, and that is suboptimal.

The upshot of all this is that if you wait until you die to have your children inherit your money, you're leaving the outcome to chance. I call it *the three Rs*—giving *random* amounts of money at a *random* time to *random* people (because who knows which of your heirs will still be alive by the time you die?). How can randomness be caring? It's the opposite of caring: Being okay with leaving all these outcomes to chance means you evidently don't care if you spend years of your life working for future random people, and it means you may not care how much the people closest to you will actually get, or when. In fact, by leaving

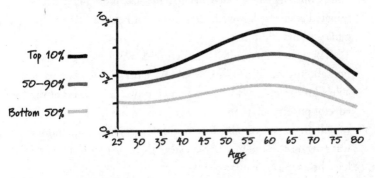

Probability of Inheritance Receipt by Income Group

For all income groups, the probability of receiving an inheritance is highest at around age 60 (2013–2016).

all these things to chance, you're even increasing the odds that whatever you've got to give will arrive too late to do much good in your kids' lives.

My colleague Marina Krakovsky, who has helped me in the research and writing of this book, read an article about a woman who was in dire financial straits, even though her mother had plenty of financial resources. Marina tracked the woman down and, well, here's what Marina found out:

For many years after her divorce, Virginia Colin struggled financially. Receiving almost no child support from her ex, she raised her four children on her own, "mostly at the edge of poverty," as she puts it. She eventually remarried, was able to hold down a decent part-time job, and attained financial stability. Then, when she was 49, her mother died, at age 76, leaving Virginia with a large inheritance: Virginia is one of five children, and each of them received $130,000. "I think the $650,000 was the maximum that you could get from one person's estate without incurring some kind of estate tax," Virginia points out, suggesting that her parents had most likely accumulated even more wealth than the total bequeathed to Virginia and her siblings.

The $130,000 windfall was definitely welcome—no question about that. "But it just would have been a lot more valuable a lot earlier," says Virginia, who is now 68. "I wasn't at the edge of poverty anymore—we weren't rich, but by this time we were living a comfortable lower-middle-class life." The money was now more like a nice bonus rather than the lifeline it would have been a decade or two earlier.

What a sad situation: Here was somebody who, for many years, barely had enough to feed herself and her children—while her parents had lots of money but, like so many others in our culture, just wanted to wait until they died to give it to her.

Virginia's parents are no longer around, so we can only guess what they would say if they heard me talking about dying with zero. If they're like most people I've spoken with, chances are they would say, "But what about the kids?"

Put Your Money Where Your Mouth Is

I know I might sound harsh when I talk about this stuff. My goal isn't to go around calling everyone a hypocrite. Most people have good intentions for themselves and for their kids—and if they're hypocrites, it's only by accident, because they fail to act on those good intentions. That's true every time you say one thing but do something else, whether or not the disconnect is deliberate. For example, in your heart of hearts, you want to enjoy your free time, but in reality you spend a good chunk of it checking your work email. Or you say you want to provide financial security for your kids, but in the end you leave it to random chance whether and how much your kids will actually get from you.

The Die with Zero way, on the other hand, makes sure that you deliver on your good intentions. It's a more thoughtful approach in both senses of the word: It simultaneously shows seriousness *and* caring. When it comes to the kids, Die with Zero shows thoughtfulness by having you put your kids first, which you do by thinking deliberately about how much to give them and then doing so, before you die.

This is radically different from how many, if not most, people in the United States approach the question of giving money to their children. Yes, some people transfer money to their kids instead of waiting until their own death—but these "in vivo" (between the living) transfers, as economists call them, make up a small minority of all wealth transfers. The vast majority—between 80 and 90 percent, depending on the year—of households that received some type of wealth transfer in the years 1989 through 2007 received an inheritance. (I'd prefer the percentage to be zero, but realistically I would be happy to see it at 20 percent, since some people die early.) And it's not at all clear whether the benefactors actually meant to leave that much to their heirs. Economists who study data on bequests say that when people leave money to their children and grandchildren, their motives appear to be some mix of intentional and unintentional. The intentional part is what you give because you want your kids to have a certain amount of money. The unintentional part is just a random by-product of precautionary saving—someone was saving money for unexpected medical expenses, for example, but ends up dying without spending all those savings, and the kids get those financial leftovers. And when economists look at the data on actual bequests, it's hard to tell whether any particular bequest was intentional or not. That's because in the end, both types of bequests look the same. All you know is that a living person got a certain amount of money from the estate of a dead person.

It's not just that economists and recipients can't tell what's intentional—what bothers me is that the givers themselves aren't really clear on this. I say that because if you are clear about your intentions, you will *not* commingle intentional gifts with unintentional ones (leftover savings) in a bequest. Instead, you will figure out what you want to give—and you will give it *well before you die.* Do you want your daughter to get $50,000 of your wealth, or only $20,000? Whatever the amount is, if your intention is to give it to her, then I encourage you to act on your positive intentions by actually giving her that amount. Be intentional with your kids just as I am urging you to be deliberate with yourself. Put your money where your mouth is.

The Enemies of Rational Thinking: Autopilot and Fear

Why don't more people act more deliberately when it comes to their kids and financial gifts? One reason is just autopilot, the antithesis of deliberate action. Autopilot is easy, and it's what most people around you are doing. So when you look around and do what everyone else is doing, you'll be coasting on autopilot just like everyone else. In fact, you might not even realize you're doing it. The sad truth is that many people aren't as deliberate as they could be with their own lives, so they're not as deliberate as they could be with their children, either.

But even if you've stopped to really think about what you want for your kids, and have the best of intentions, you've got to overcome another powerful force pushing against rational thought and deliberate action: fear. This is exactly what kept Virginia Colin's parents from sharing their wealth when she was on the edge of poverty. "My dad grew up as the son of an immigrant from Germany, during the Depression," Virginia explained, "and he was afraid of not having enough even when they had more than enough. What if there was a huge, expensive medical problem?"

As it turned out, Virginia's father did live into his nineties —outliving Virginia's mother—but although he had some big medical problems, private insurance and Medicare covered most of the cost.

I know that's easy to say in retrospect. Maybe he was just lucky. What if he'd had a particularly costly disease, like Alzheimer's, which typically requires expensive long-term care? Wouldn't he have needed his savings for that? As noted earlier, if that's the main reason you feel compelled to keep saving and saving, remember that you can buy long-term care insurance, which costs far less than self-insuring by saving massive amounts of money for a crisis that may never come. Just like any other kind of insurance.

In any case, Virginia learned from her parents' experience: Don't wait until you're dead to give your money away. With her five children and stepchildren, ranging in age from 29 to 43, she and her husband make a point of giving them money sooner rather than later, depending on their needs. "If you get [the money] when you are 30," she rightly points out, "you can buy a nice house and raise your kids in the environment you want to raise them in, and not have to scramble the way I did."

Timing Is Everything

As Virginia's story illustrates, timing is key. We've already estab-
lished that waiting until you die is not optimal—so what is the
optimal time to give money to your children?

Certainly it's easier to say what is suboptimal. Most people who have assets to give to children wouldn't give them to a
12-year-old, or even a 16-year-old. It's pretty obvious that children and most teens are too young to manage wealth.

But of course that doesn't equate to "the later the better." I
don't want to say there's an age when it's just too late to give your
children money—late, after all, is better than never—but age
60 is worse than 50, and 50 is worse than 40. Why? Because a
person's ability to extract real enjoyment out of the gift declines
with their age. This happens for exactly the same reason your
own ability to convert money into enjoyable experiences diminishes after you get past a certain age. And for a whole host of activities, you need a certain minimum mental and physical state
to enjoy them at all.

So, for example, if the *peak utility of money* (the time when
it can bring optimal usefulness or enjoyment) occurs at age 30,
then at age 30 every dollar buys you one dollar's worth of enjoyment. By age 50, the utility of money has declined consider-
ably: Either you would get a lot less enjoyment out of that same
dollar or you would need more money (say, $1.50) to obtain the
same amount of enjoyment as you got out of $1 back when you
were a healthy, vibrant 30-year-old. For the same reason, as your
adult children age, every dollar you give them goes less far, and
at some point that money becomes almost useless to them.

Let's look at a more specific example. Suppose you ignore my advice about giving money to your kids before you die, and you want to take the more traditional route of leaving some money to your children after you die. Now assume that your life expectancy is 86, and that your oldest child is 28 years younger than you—so they'll be 58 when you die and they inherit. At this point, they're well past their peak of extracting enjoyment out of that money. Now, I don't know the exact age of this peak, but based on what I know about human physiology and mental growth, between the ages of 26 and 35 seems about right, and 58 is clearly past that optimal point.

I actually did an informal Twitter poll recently in which I asked people what their ideal age was to receive an inheritance windfall, and most of them agreed. Of the more than 3,500 people who voted on this question, very few (only 6 percent) said the ideal age to inherit money is 46 or older. Another 29 percent voted for ages 36 to 45, while only 12 percent said 18 to 25. The clear winner, with more than half the votes, was the age range 26 to 35. Why? Well, some people mentioned the time value of money and the power of compound interest, suggesting that the earlier you get the money, the better. On the other hand, a bunch of people pointed out the immaturity problem of getting the money too young. And to those two concerns, I would add the element of health: You always get more value out of money *before* your health begins to inevitably decline. Bottom line? The 26-to-35 age range combines the best of all these considerations —old enough to be trusted with money, yet young enough to fully enjoy its benefits.

What I'm pointing out is the stark contrast between what people say they want . . . and what the U.S. inheritance data shows most people actually get. You can't always get what you want—but I'm talking to *you* as the prospective giver. If you have the means to give money to your children, then you have the power to control when they receive it. So don't waste that opportunity! Whatever you give your heirs past their optimal age of receiving has less value to them. If you're trying to maximize the impact of the money you give—instead of just maximizing the absolute dollar amount you give—then you should aim to give the money as close to their peak as you can.

Now, you might disagree with me about the right age to begin to turn assets over to your kids. But even so, you must acknowledge the decreasing value to your offspring with respect to time. Just take it to the extreme: the case of your leaving money after living a very long life. Does it make sense to wait and leave money to a 76-year-old? No, most people would say that's too old. (My friend Baird has a mother who's 76 and knows she can't spend her money before she dies—the last trip she took lasted five days, and that was two days too long, he says. Since her money is of limited use to her, she has been trying to give it away to Baird, who is 50—but by this point, Baird really doesn't need the money anymore!)

Optimization doesn't care whether we're talking about parents or children: The same principles, such as the declining value of money, apply to everyone. If your goal is to maximize what you get out of your life, it makes sense to want to maximize what your kids get out of their lives, too. So if you want to make the most of your gifts to your kids, you have to consider each recipient's age. By applying this line of thinking, you will be taking money that is nonproductive in terms of life enjoyment and turning it into money that is maximally useful.

This is exactly what I'm trying to do with my own kids. For my daughters, who are not yet 25, I've funded an educational savings plan (a 529 plan) and set up a trust. Mind you, the money in the trust is their money, not mine, and I contribute to it as I see fit, up to the maximum that I'm willing to give. My stepson is older—29—so he's already received 90 percent of his "inheritance," in the form of money he used to buy a house. (By the way, spreading out your giving in this way is totally fine. But I sure am not going to wait until he's 65 to give him the rest!)

I do have a will, which is only for disposing of what I have in case I die unexpectedly. A while ago I realized I had money in my will for people who are older than me—my mom and my sister and my brother. That made me think: *What about now? Do I want to give anything* now, *when they can enjoy those gifts more than later?* My answer was yes, so I gave them that amount.

In short, by giving the money to my kids and other people at a time when it can have the greatest impact on their lives, I'm making it their money, not mine. That's a clear distinction, and I find it liberating: It frees me to spend to the hilt on myself. If I want to spend like mad, I can do it without worrying about the effect on my kids. They have their money to spend as they wish, and I have mine.

Your Real Legacy Isn't Money

I spent much of this chapter talking about giving your money to your offspring—but that's only because money is what most people are talking about when they ask, "What about the kids?" But remember, money is just a means to an end—a way to buy the meaningful experiences that make up your life. As I explained in chapter 2, I'm assuming that your goal in life is *not* to maximize your income and wealth but to maximize your lifetime fulfillment, which comes from experiences and your lasting memories of those experiences. And just as you're trying to maximize your own fulfillment, you're trying to maximize your children's fulfillment too.

The same holds for memories: Just as you're trying to form memories of times with your kids, it makes sense to want your kids to form memories of you. Both sets of memories will yield a memory dividend—one stream of dividends for you and one for your kids. So how do you want your kids to remember you? That's just another way of asking: What kinds of experiences do you want them to have with you?

That's important to think about before it's too late. Look at it from the perspective of the child deprived of experiences with the parent. A friend of mine received a massive fortune from his father, with whom he had almost no relationship while growing up, because the dad was always away chasing deals to build his fortune. So despite the family's impressive wealth, my friend had a pretty miserable childhood. He was the classic poor little rich boy. The years of emotional neglect put a lasting strain on the father-son relationship: When the two did finally have time together, they found that they had trouble enjoying each other's company. There was just no way to make up for all that lost time and attention. Now when my friend thinks of his father's legacy, material wealth is one of the few things he recalls with any sense of gratitude.

It's like the song "Cat's in the Cradle." The lyrics are just heartbreaking: The man telling the story basically missed his son's whole childhood, because there were always "planes to catch and bills to pay."

A lot of people quote from "Cat's in the Cradle" because it is so emotionally moving and rings true for so many people who hear it. I love the song, too, with its message that you can't delay experiences with your kids indefinitely—but its message is incomplete. Yes, many of us are too busy chasing x, y, and z for the sake of future benefits, not realizing that the time to have meaningful experiences with our children is now. But it's too simplistic to leave it at that, because there's a limit to the benefits of spending additional time with your kids. You can't delay everything, but you can delay some things.

I do believe firmly that your real legacy for your kids consists of the experiences you've shared with your children, especially when they're growing up—the lessons and other memories you've imparted to them. But I don't mean it in a schmaltzy, best-things-in-life-are-free way. In fact, the best things in life aren't actually free, because everything you do takes away from something else you could be doing. Spending time with your family usually means *not* spending that time earning money—and the other way around. Instead, there are ways to think about experiences in a more quantitative way that will help you make better decisions about how to spend your time.

But before I get to that, let me make my main point clear: Of all the experiences you are trying to bequeath to your child, one of those experiences is time with you.

Time with you is crucial, because the memories your kids have of you have lasting effects, for better or worse. Scientists have known for some time that young adults who as young children receive more affection from their parents come to enjoy better personal relationships in general and to also have lower rates of substance abuse and depression. We also know that the positive effects of loving, attentive parents last well past young adulthood, thanks to a study of more than 7,000 middle-aged adults. Researchers asked these adults a bunch of questions about their memories of their mother and father—questions like "How much time and attention did she/he give you when you needed it?" and "How much did she/he teach you about life?" and "How would you rate your relationship with your mother/ father during the years you were growing up?"

Obviously, the higher a person's ratings on questions like these, the more positive their childhood memories of that parent. So what did the researchers find? By correlating these ratings with answers to questions about particular outcomes, the researchers were able to conclude that those adults who had memories of higher parental affection ended up with better health and lower levels of depression. The word "experience" may not evoke images of a child being taught about life, or of simply being given time and attention—but all those are indeed experiences, too, and they're indispensable, paying off in sometimes surprising ways. I don't know anybody who wouldn't want that kind of experience and that kind of memory dividend for their children.

So how do you quantify such things—what is the value of a positive memory? Your first instinct might be to say that it's impossible to say, or that memories are priceless. But let me put it another way: What is the value to you of a week at a cabin on a lake? Or of a day with a beloved relative? The price might be extremely high or fairly low, but the fact that you can even propose a ballpark price says that the value of an experience can be quantified. (In fact, you might recall doing that with "experience points" in an earlier chapter.)

I am making a big deal about quantifying the value of experiences with your children because doing so forces you to pause and think about what's *really* best for your kids: Sometimes it is earning more money, and sometimes it is spending more time with them. So many people tell themselves that they are working for their kids—they just blindly assume that earning more money will benefit their kids. But until you stop to think about the numbers, you can't know whether sacrificing your time to earn more money will result in a net benefit for your children.

What can thinking about the numbers tell you? Well, take an extreme example. Let's say you live in the wilderness, and you must "go to work" to cut down trees just to build a basic shelter for your family. When you have to work just to enable your family to survive, of course it makes sense to work instead of hanging out with them. But once you get past the point of just working for basic needs and avoiding negative experiences, you can start to exchange your labor for positive life experiences. As far as your children are concerned, you can either work for more money to buy them experiences or spend your extra free time to give them the experience of time with you.

At the other extreme is the billionaire who works such long hours and travels so much for work that he spends no time at all with his children. If you're already a billionaire, it's safe to assume that your children would be better off if you spent at least a little more time with them, even if it's to the detriment of your career. The financial cost to your career is small, but the benefit to your children is immense. So it's a net gain to the family, including to you.

The value of time with your kids is like the value of water —if you've got 50 gallons of water, you wouldn't pay a dime for an additional gallon of water. But if you're dying of thirst in the desert, you might be willing to cut off your arm to get even one gallon.

Most of us, of course, are somewhere between these two extremes. We are neither working all the time just to survive nor completely neglecting our children. As such, we are facing a more difficult trade-off between time and money. But the thought process should be the same as at the extremes, even if the answer isn't obvious: Is each additional hour of work you do really worth it to you and your children? Does your work add to your legacy—or does it actually serve to deplete it?

Parents' employment is a mixed blessing for kids of all income levels. When parents go to work, the income they earn can improve their kids' lives in many ways, but as the economist Carolyn Heinrich points out, work (especially long hours and night shifts) can take time away from parent-child bonding and can bring real stress into children's lives. And low-income parents are especially likely to be working stressful jobs with long hours. But, of course, most people have to work to provide for their families, and the optimal balance between time at work and time with your kids isn't always obvious.

Where you and your children are in your lives matters, too. Just as you can't keep delaying ski trips because there is a minimum level of basic health you need in order to go skiing, you can't keep delaying time with your six-year-old, because eventually your child won't be six. Or seven. Or a child. The fact that those opportunities gradually disappear should cause you to reevaluate how much money you'd be willing to give up to have those experiences.

Now look at it from your kids' point of view, because it's our kids' fulfillment that we're trying to maximize here. What do you suppose is the value to your child of an extra day with you? Or to have you home when she comes home from school? Or to have you attend her soccer game or music recital? I'm well aware that your kids, especially when they're very young, probably don't value these experiences when they're having them. If

I were to ask my older daughter how much she values my going to one of her games, she might not even know what I was talking about. But these shared experiences clearly have a value, especially in retrospect. Remember: The purpose of money is to have experiences, and one of those experiences for your kids is time with you. Therefore, if you are earning money but not having experiences with your kids, you are actually depriving your kids. And yourself.

If you really think through the implications of saying that your legacy consists of experiences with your children, the conclusion you reach might be somewhat radical: That is, once you have enough money to take care of your family's basic needs, then by going to work to earn more money, you might actually be depleting your kids' inheritance because you are spending less time with them! And the richer you already are, the more likely this is to be true.

Charity Can't Wait

Guess what! Almost everything I've said about giving money to your kids at the right time applies to donations to charity. Whether the money or time you're giving is to children, to charity, or to yourself, the key concept is the same: There is an optimal time, and it is never when you're dead.

Consider this headline, above one of the most emailed *New York Times* stories in the week it came out: "96-Year-Old Secretary Quietly Amasses Fortune, Then Donates $8.2 Million." Wow! The story explained how a Brooklyn woman named Sylvia Bloom managed to amass so much wealth on her salary as a legal secretary. Though she'd been married, she had no children, and she worked for the same Wall Street law firm for 67 years, lived in a rent-controlled apartment, took the subway to work even into her nineties—and made her savings grow by replicating on a smaller scale the investments made by the lawyers she worked for.

Nobody close to Ms. Bloom had any idea of her wealth until after her death. She made a bequest of $6.24 million to a social service organization called the Henry Street Settlement; another $2 million went to Hunter College and a scholarship fund. Everyone at the Settlement was blown away. Bloom's niece, who was the organization's treasurer, was especially stunned. It was the largest single gift from an individual in the organization's 125-year-history. The group's executive director called the gift "the epitome of selflessness."

Now, I understand where he's coming from—it does seem selfless to leave so much money after living on so little, and a good deed is a good deed—but in all candor, I don't see Bloom's actions as the height of selflessness.

You Can't Be Generous When You're Dead

Before I explain why Bloom's actions don't seem all that selfless, let me explain that I can't say whether someone's decision is good or bad, rational or irrational, without knowing what the person wants. For example, I personally might prefer to give my time and money to people rather than to animals—but if someone would rather volunteer at an animal rescue than a homeless shelter, who am I to say that's irrational? As long as what they do is consistent with what they actually want, I have to respect their decision even if it's not the decision I would have made. There's just no accounting for taste.

Therefore, I can't say that Sylvia Bloom made a mistake in working her whole life and scrimping to eventually have all that money go to someone else. We can only guess whether she was denying herself deliberately to give a larger gift to others (which would indeed be generous) or whether she was just living on autopilot, with her beneficiaries getting whatever was left (which would not be generous). Why? Well, once you're dead, the transfer of your assets is legally enforced, and the only say you have in the matter (through your will, obviously created before you die) is where those assets get transferred. But your money is taken no matter what—so how can that be generous? The dead don't pay taxes—only the recipients of their bequests do. So you can be generous only when you're alive, when you have actual choices and their consequences: That's when you can choose whether to give your money or your time to one thing or another. If you give generously when you're alive, then I can consider you selfless. If you're dead, you just don't have that choice. So by definition, you cannot be generous when you're dead.

A Terrible Inefficiency

Maybe you think I'm splitting hairs about the meaning of selflessness, generosity, and choice. Bloom did, after all, scrimp and save and put those charities in her will, so she must have had generous intentions, right? Okay. And it's possible that she also received a lot of joy from saving that money with the knowledge that someday it would go to a cause she cared about—charitable giving, after all, is another way to have an experience.

So what's the problem? The problem is terrible inefficiency: People who were needy during her lifetime did not benefit from her largesse. Here was a person who, by her own choice to consume very little of her growing wealth, routinely lived far below her means. She chose to keep taking the subway to work and to keep living in a rent-controlled apartment (which, incidentally, could have gone to a needier person). Let's assume that she was saving specifically so that her money could go to these charities. So why didn't she give it to her beloved charities earlier, when she clearly could have?

Well, maybe part of her motive for saving was precautionary —she might have thought there was a good chance she would need to spend $2 million at 72 to take care of herself. Or maybe she thought of the money growing in her accounts as some sort of score, a measure of how well she was doing, instead of a way to have an impact on the world. Or maybe she didn't really think it through; after all, large grants at death are a deeply ingrained part of our culture. I don't know—we can only guess. But I do know that her delay was inefficient, because her charities certainly could have put the money to use earlier, benefiting many more people sooner.

Think, for example, of the amazing gift Robert F. Smith gave to the class of 2019 of Morehouse College, paying off all their student loans. Whatever his motives were, whatever amount his gift added up to, the point is that Smith didn't put it in his will —he gave while he was still very much alive, enabling *today's* graduates to leave college debt-free.

Sylvia Bloom, too, gave to educational causes, which is particularly interesting for our purposes, because the benefits of investing in education are so well documented. The benefits accrue not just to individual students (who, as a result of education, can get better jobs and enjoy better health) but also to society as a whole. Lower rates of poverty and lower rates of crime and violence are just the most obvious social benefits of education. Economists have also tried quantifying the return on investment in education, finding that, worldwide, the social returns to schooling at the secondary and higher education levels are above 10 percent (per year). What other investment can yield such a reliably high rate of return? To justify holding on to the money and investing it on your own rather than giving it to your favorite educational charity now, you'd have to know that you can earn more than that rate of return year after year. Charitable organizations certainly prefer to get your money now. But some charities, particularly foundations and endowed nonprofits, don't use the money they receive right away, either; instead, they aim to grow their endowments by taking in more than they give away each year. For example, in 1999, foundations took in more than $90 billion but distributed less than $25 billion. That is why one analysis concludes that "donors should ask not just how, but how soon, their gifts will be used." I couldn't agree more. But no matter how your favorite charity spends your money, the charity always gets more out of having the money sooner.

Your Legacy Is Now

You already know my take on timing your spending in general: that it's important. My number one rule is: Maximize your life experiences. So spend your money while you're alive—whether it's on yourself, your loved ones, or charity. And beyond that, find the optimal times to spend money.

When it comes to giving money to your kids, the optimal

time, as I suggested earlier in the chapter, is when they're between 26 and 35—not too late to make a big impact and not so soon that they might squander the money. But what about giving money to charity? With charity, there's no such thing as too soon. The sooner you give money to medical research, for example, the sooner that money can help combat disease—as we can see from the research into returns on investments in medical research. Every day, a new technological advancement happens that improves lives, and over time these advances make a huge difference. But you can't just wait for these things to happen—you have to give what you can based on the resources you have today and the resources you expect to have in the future.

A friend of mine was telling me he wants to start a business, and if the business succeeds he wants to give the proceeds to charity. His goal with the business is to create a huge charitable impact. You can probably guess what I told him: that his charity needs his money now. If you have the money now to invest in a new business, and your whole point of investing in the business is to earn money for charity, you and the charity would both be better off if you just gave them your money right now—even if it's less than what you might be able to give later. The suffering is happening now, so the time to start relieving it is now, not at some distant date in the future.

More and more philanthropists are taking this approach, which billionaire philanthropist Chuck Feeney calls "giving while living." Feeney, who made his fortune as a founder of Duty Free Shoppers Group (the duty-free stores you see in airports), is a great role model for what I'm advocating: He started giving his money away (anonymously) early, and by the time he was in his eighties he had given away more than $8 billion of his wealth. He had chosen to live frugally, like legal secretary Sylvia

Bloom—but unlike Bloom, he didn't wait until his death for that money to go to charitable causes. He's now in his eighties, and by choice he and his wife live in a rented apartment. His net worth is now down to about $2 million—still plenty to sustain him for the rest of his life, but a tiny fraction of the money he gave away over the years.

Feeney has been an inspiration to many wealthy people, including Bill Gates and Warren Buffett. But you don't have to be rich to give while living. The same principle applies at any scale, whether you have billions, thousands, or hundreds. It doesn't take much money to make a noticeable impact on people in the developing world: Through organizations like Save the Children and Compassion International, you can sponsor a child for less than $500 per year, helping the child grow up safe, healthy, and better educated—and starting a positive cycle for future generations.

If you don't have as much money to give away as you'd like, you still probably have *time* to give. So remember, when I say "die with zero," I don't mean die with the money that you're going to give to charity. If you plan to give, give while you're alive, and the earlier the better. Your charity can't wait.

Recommendations

- Consider at what ages you want to give money to your children, and how much you want to give. The same goes with giving money to charity. Discuss these issues with your spouse or partner. And do it today!
- Be sure to consult on these matters with an expert such as an estate planner or a lawyer as well.

6

BALANCE YOUR LIFE

Rule No. 6:
Don't live your life on autopilot.

At the beginning of this book, I told you about the time my boss told me I was an idiot. As you might recall, I was a penny-pinching guy in my twenties, proud of myself for managing to save up money on my meager salary. My boss, Joe Farrell, knocked some sense into me by reminding me that I was on a path to earn much more in the coming years, so I was foolish not to spend whatever money I was making now.

Joe Farrell didn't just make this advice up. The idea that it's rational for young people to be freer with their money is shared by many economists, even though it runs counter to the advice most of us grow up hearing. When we're around eight or nine years old, our parents tell us to save some of our birthday money instead of spending it all. When we're all grown up, financial advisers tell us it's never too early to start saving part of our paychecks.

Many economists, on the other hand, think that thrift among young people is generally a bad idea. When economist Steven Levitt, of *Freakonomics* fame, landed at the University of Chicago as a first-year professor, a senior colleague named José Scheinkman told him he should spend more and save less—the same advice that Scheinkman himself had gotten from Milton Friedman, the even more famous University of Chicago economist. "Your salary will only go up, your earning power will only go up," Levitt recalls his older colleague telling him, in almost a perfect echo of what Joe Farrell told me. "And so you shouldn't be saving now, you should be borrowing. You should be living today in much the way that you'll be living in 10 or 15 years, and it's crazy to actually be scrimping and saving, which is what at least someone like me who was brought up in a middle-class family was taught to do." Levitt says this was one of the best pieces of financial advice he ever got.

I'd say the same thing about the nearly identical advice Joe Farrell gave me, even though for a time I took it too far. Joe's words opened my eyes to a whole new way of thinking about balancing your earnings with your spending. I was like a zealous convert—there was the me before that talk with Joe, and a very different me after. Before, I had been living much the way people in the FIRE movement are living today—doing everything on the cheap, watching every penny, and saving as much as I possibly could for the future. Then Joe's words flipped a switch in me. Real fast, I swung from being a FIRE guy to a guy basically lighting money on fire. In the next few years, my income kept rising, as Joe had said it would, and my spending kept rising, too.

I was having a lot of fun, but unfortunately I can't point to a particular experience I had in those years that yielded much of a memory dividend. That's because I was going bananas—just spending money to spend money, instead of being selective. For example, I'd buy a stereo system with a higher sound fidelity than my ears could perceive, or I'd go to restaurants that were more expensive but not that different from the restaurants I'd dined at before. Basically, if there was a more expensive version of something, I'd go for it without thinking about getting the maximum value. In effect, I just went from autopilot-save to autopilot-spend.

My spending also jeopardized my future. I wasn't just spending all my discretionary income; I was also cutting deep into my emergency safety stash. What if I lost my job? Besides unemployment insurance, I'd have no cushion to lean on—not even one month's salary.

I'm still a big believer in taking risks when you're young enough to recover from the possible downside—but only if there's an upside, a reward that makes the risk pay off. It's always got to be risk/reward. So if I were going to Nepal, for example, to take a journey I'd never get to take again because later I'd have kids and other responsibilities, then that's a risk worth taking. It'd be okay to spend all I had and even go into debt (like my friend Jason did for his backpacking trip through Europe) for that kind of once-in-a-lifetime experience. I wouldn't call that lighting money on fire. But my spending at that time wasn't anything like that: For what I was getting, the risk I was taking wasn't worth it.

But you see why I went too far: In trying to avoid my earlier idiocy of depriving myself, I just became a different kind of idiot. In taking Joe's wisdom and running with it, I was replacing one mistake with another: Earlier I was too thrifty, and later I was too spendthrift. The real wisdom of Joe's advice isn't to always spend everything you earn and to keep betting on an ever brighter future. No, the key takeaway, I now realize, is to *strike the right balance between spending on the present (and only on what you value) and saving smartly for the future.*

Why Simple Balance Rules
Don't Work for Everyone

I've also come to realize that this balance keeps shifting as you move through your life. That's also quite contrary to most personal finance advice. For example, some financial experts urge you to save "at least 10 percent" of your income each month or each paycheck. Other experts will suggest other numbers, like 20 percent—but again, they suggest you do this every month or week or paycheck, regardless of your age or financial situation.

Let's look at the 20 percent recommendation, which comes from a popular budgeting formula called the 50-30-20 rule. 50-30-20 comes from Elizabeth Warren—yes, that same Elizabeth Warren. Before she entered politics, Warren had been a law professor with special expertise in bankruptcy and also co-wrote books about why middle-class Americans go broke and how to avoid that dismal fate. She suggested the 50-30-20 rule, which she called the Balanced Money Formula, as a way to help people maintain financial stability.

According to this rule, you should budget 50 percent of your income for must-haves (like rent, groceries, and utilities), 30 percent for your personal wants (like travel, entertainment, and dining out), and the remaining 20 percent on building your savings and paying down your debt. The rule sounds like a great (and simple) way to achieve that goal, especially for people who may not have a good grip on their spending. It certainly caught on. But if you want to go beyond financial stability—that is, if you share my goal of maximizing your lifetime fulfillment without going broke—then you'll need a more sophisticated way of thinking about balance. To my way of thinking, no way can the same ratio of spending to saving be right for everyone—and, more important, no way should your savings percentage be the same when you're 22 as when you're 42 or 52. The optimal balance will vary from person to person and will shift as your age and income change. This chapter will show you several methods to help you find and maintain that optimal balance for yourself.

Why the Spend-Save Balance Keeps Shifting

The 50-30-20 rule and other simple formulas suggest a constant ratio of spending to savings. For example, in the 50-30-20 rule, in which you save 20 percent of your income, the ratio is 80 to 20. If you take out the must-haves, meaning that the only spending you count is on wants (more or less what I call "experiences"), the ratio of spending to saving is 30 to 20. Why do I say that such a balance can't be right throughout your life? Because it's not an optimal allocation of your life energy. You already understand part of the reason if you agree with Joe Farrell and Steve

Levitt: It's crazy to save 20 percent of your income when you're young and have good reason to expect to earn much more in the next few years.

In fact, as Levitt suggests, it can even make sense to borrow money (spending more than you're currently earning) when you expect to earn a lot more down the road.

And just to be clear: When I say it makes sense to borrow money when you're young, I'm *not* saying you should be racking up credit card debt—such high-interest loans are a bad idea for almost everyone. Borrow modestly and responsibly. And when you have many years of rising income ahead of you, it really doesn't make sense to save 20 percent of your income. That would mean forgoing memorable life experiences you could be having, and it also means working to pay for a richer future self —a suboptimal use of your life energy, that's for sure.

Okay, suppose you agree with me that a balance of 80 to 20 is suboptimal for many young workers. But what about older workers? Obviously, at some point you will have to start saving for your retirement, when you'll otherwise have little to no income. And it's not just retirement you need to save for—there will almost always come times in your life when your income will hit a plateau, or your spending will need to rise, or both will happen at the same time. For all those eventualities, you do need to save money at some point, no doubt about it. When that time comes, you don't want to save too much (because you'd be forgoing experiences you may never have again), and you don't want to save too little, either (because that would deprive your future self). You want to save as close to the perfect amount as possible: You want to achieve the optimal balance between enjoying the present and providing for a good future.

But even when you do reach an age when it's wise to start saving, there will *not* be one magic number, an ideal constant savings rate that will keep you in balance until you retire. To understand why, you need to fully understand a concept I touched on earlier: A person's ability to extract enjoyment from their money begins to decline with age. What does this mean? The idea becomes crystal clear when you look at a person on their deathbed. Too weak and fragile to move their body, perhaps needing a feeding tube and a bedpan for some of their most basic functions, the person on their deathbed can't do much of anything except think back to what they've already done in their life. You can give them a private jet to anywhere in the world—but they're just not going anywhere. Whether they've saved up a million dollars or a billion, the money won't make a real difference in increasing their enjoyment of what they've got left in life. Admittedly, this is a grim way of looking at the end of one's years. But it does put everything into sharp focus. At this point in life, the only person with less ability to extract enjoyment from money is the one in the morgue or the grave.

What does that have to do with you as a healthy 40-year-old or however old you are now? Everything! I often think about these deathbed scenarios because the fact that we all will die has implications for every day of our lives. We've all heard the hypothetical question "What would you do if you knew you were going to die tomorrow?" The person asking this question often follows your answer with "Why don't you do these things now?" Well, the obvious answer is that you probably will *not* die tomorrow, so it's foolish to act as if you will. In general, when you will die should affect how you spend your time.

As I mentioned earlier, if you knew you were going to die tomorrow, you'd spend today one way, and if it was two days from now, you would spend today slightly differently—because you'll still have tomorrow. The same is true for three days from now, four days from now, or 20,000 days from now: The further back in time you go, the more the balance shifts between living for today and planning for the future. So if you work your way back one day or year at a time, from your deathbed to the wheelchair to retirement, and then further back to your thirties, twenties, and so on, you should see at least subtle changes in how you should be spending your life. This is easy to see when you're talking about a few days—those changes aren't subtle. But when we're talking about *thousands* of days—of years and decades—people tend to forget this logic altogether and act as if 20,000 days is the same as forever. But of course none of us have forever. We need to keep that in mind so that we take optimal advantage of the time we have and don't fall into the trap of living our lives on autopilot.

Travel is a good example: To me, travel is the ultimate gauge of a person's ability to extract enjoyment from money, because it takes time, money, and, above all, health. Many 80-year-olds just can't travel much or far—their health prevents it. But you don't need to be completely debilitated to want to avoid some of the hassles associated with travel. The less healthy you are, the less you're able to cope with long flights, airport layovers, irregular sleep, and other travel-related stressors. A study of people's travel constraints—what kept them from traveling to a specific destination—not only confirms this intuition but goes further. Some researchers asked people of different ages what prevented them from taking a trip. They found that people under age 60 are most constrained by time and money, whereas people 75 and older are most constrained by health problems. In other words, when time and money are no longer a problem, health is. And it's not as if there comes one age at which people suddenly start having health problems that prevent them from traveling. "Health problems were increasingly a constraint as age increased," the researchers reported, "and were a major constraint to the oldest respondents."

It's a harsh reality: Your health just keeps declining from your peak years in your late teens and twenties, sometimes suddenly but usually so gradually that you don't notice it. When I was young, I loved playing sports, especially football. I still like football—but even as a healthy 50-year-old, I can't possibly enjoy it as much as I did when I was 20. I can't run as fast, and I'm much more prone to injuries. When you're afraid of tearing a rotator cuff or busting your knee, football just isn't as much fun. Friends who are around my age agree: At a certain point, your memories of having played football are a lot more pleasant than playing football.

This happens with all kinds of physical activities. Last week, I was playing tennis and noticed that my knees were kind of hurting, so I stopped. That wouldn't have happened 20 years ago. My friend Greg, who loves skiing and is in great shape (for his age), recently went skiing for seven days in a row—something he could have done easily when he was 22—but afterwards he was in a lot of pain and realized that skiing seven days straight is too much for him now.

This diminished enjoyment from declining health also has a real impact on how far your dollar goes, and skiing is a good example of this effect. Let's say that an aging skier decides to continue enjoying the sport by giving himself more breaks or longer breaks between runs. Great idea—but that doesn't mean he's getting the same experience as when he was younger and stronger. If he used to get in 20 good runs in one day on the slopes, now he can manage only 15. In effect, the same amount of money he spent on that day of skiing now brings him only 75 percent of the skiing enjoyment it did years earlier.

My buddy Greg will recover and be able to ski again, but his future enjoyment will be diminished because he can't ski as much as he used to—and eventually not at all.

I am reminded of this sad reality all the time because many people I know are noticing similar physical constraints sneaking up on them. I'll tell you a particularly dramatic example. In the British Virgin Islands, on an island called Jost Van Dyke, there's a great spot on the beach called the Soggy Dollar Bar. It has that name because there's no dock; people anchor their boats a little ways offshore and literally swim up to the bar, paying for their famous Painkiller cocktail with wet dollars. Some people prefer to catch a ride on the back of a Seabob, which they can do, but if you like swimming, you get to have the full wet-dollar experience.

Well, that's what my girlfriend's granddad, Chris (aged 69 at the time), wanted to do when he came out to visit—he's a former swim coach and was raring to go, so in he and I went, into the water. It's a short swim, 30 yards or so, but about 20 yards in I heard Chris yell, "How much further?" I yelled back that he could stand (the water was shallow), but he didn't hear me. When I got to him, he was breathing uncontrollably! I quickly thought about CPR, and whether we could get a defibrillator in time if this went south fast. Luckily, it didn't come to that—Chris started to regain his composure, and after 15 minutes his breathing and heart rate were normal, so he and I were able to enjoy a Painkiller with our soggy dollars. Phew!

Chris and many others remember their glory days without noticing what is happening to their bodies—in Chris's case, that he was not in shape to swim 30 yards. Many of us have this mental disconnect with reality, and the disconnect helps perpetuate the myth of endless go-go years in retirement, as if we'll always be able to do what we enjoy doing.

Now, you might be saying, "That might be true for many people, but I'm in better shape than I was 20 years ago!" Well, to me that just says that you weren't taking great care of your health earlier—because if you were, you definitely would have been in better shape 20 years ago. All other things being equal, a 20-year-old is healthier and stronger than a 40-year-old, and a 55-year-old is healthier and stronger than a 75-year-old. Those are just physical facts of life. Let me show you some evidence from medical research.

Different systems in your body deteriorate at different rates —but they all deteriorate. For example, when medical researchers track a population's changes in bone density and muscle mass over time, they report different sets of numbers for the two measures. To complicate matters, they also find significant differences between groups of people. White females, for example, have lower bone density in their hips than do black females, and both groups have lower bone density than black males do. But all groups show a decline with age.

Researchers also track different indicators of eye health (visual function), such as contrast sensitivity, retinal thickness, and visual acuity. Lung function has its own trajectory of decline with age. So do cardiac health, cognitive function, and sense of smell, among many others. So there are many different health curves, not just one, and they all look somewhat different: Some decline in a steady, almost linear trajectory, while others are more curved, showing an accelerating rate of decline. Also, group differences aside, some individuals are healthier than others to begin with, and some are better at maintaining their health over time, so ranges are more telling than single curves are. But no matter what specific health data you look at or how many curves you combine, 80-year-olds are *a lot* less healthy than 25-year-olds.

To some extent, the rate of physical health decline is up to you. The better you maintain your health, the less steep your decline. For example, the lung-function curve for nonsmokers is a lot flatter than the curve for smokers. The better your health in a given year, the more you will be able to enjoy your experiences that year. So, yes, you will decline—but you have a say in the shape of the decline! That's a good thing, because the better you're able to maintain your health during your lifetime, the higher your lifetime fulfillment score will be. But don't kid yourself: No matter how much you take care of your body, you will not be in better health at 65 than you were at 25, assuming you were in normal health as a 25-year-old.

On a personal level, I've become even more deliberate in my decisions about what to do and when. The other day my friends and I rented a boat and I thought about wakeboarding, which is like snowboarding on water. At age 50, was I still in good enough shape to do it? Probably. Would I be in good enough shape seven years from now? Definitely not. This activity had to happen now or never, so I decided to go for it. I don't want to get to the end of my days, when I no longer have my health, and realize there were things I wanted to do that I didn't do earlier, when I was able to.

Your ability to enjoy many experiences in life depends on your health—but money plays a part, too, because a lot of activities cost money. So you'd better spend the money when you still have the health.

Here's the point: Too many of us still view ourselves on an

ongoing basis as being in our twenties, even though our real age is somewhere in our fifties, sixties, or even seventies. While it's admirable to view oneself as "young at heart," it's also necessary to be more realistic and objective about your body and how it's aging. You *have* to be mindful and aware of your physical limits, and how they are steadily encroaching upon you as you get older, whether you like it or not.

I first started thinking about these things after that time I gave my grandmother $10,000 and discovered she just couldn't spend it. All she really wanted to buy at that point was a sweater for me. I started noticing the same kind of thing with other older relatives, and I thought, *These are my ancestors, so I'm probably going to be that person, too, at some point.* And it occurred to me that *everybody* becomes like that eventually. As you get older, your health declines and your interests gradually narrow, just as your sex drive diminishes. Your creativity usually declines, too. And when you're extremely old and frail, no matter what your level of interest is, just about all you can do is sit and eat tapioca pudding. At that point, money is useless to you, because all you need or want is to lie in bed and watch *Jeopardy.* This was my conclusion: The utility, or usefulness, of money declines with age.

It was also clear to me that the decline doesn't start from birth. When we're infants, we get very little enjoyment out of money. Babies are expensive to take care of, true, but it's not like they get a lot of enjoyment from spending money. When you're a baby, there's no greater happiness than Mom and the crib. In a way, the amount of utility that babies get from money is very similar to what the elderly get. Money is nearly worthless at the very beginning and the very end of life.

What happens in between? When I was back in my twenties,

I could always find new things to do with money. Cash in your twenties has a lot of utility. So when I looked at these three points —the baby, the twenty-something, and the old person—I realized that *there must be a curve*. In other words, if the horizontal axis on a graph represents your age, and the vertical axis represents your capacity to enjoy life experiences that money can buy, then if you were to plot your potential enjoyment by age, you would see some kind of curve. Think of it this way: Given the same amount of money each year (let's say $100,000), you will be able to extract a lot more enjoyment out of that money at some points in your life than at others. The utility of money changes over time, and it does so in a fairly predictable way: Starting sometime in your twenties, your health very subtly starts to decline, causing a corresponding decline in your ability to enjoy money.

This thought immediately suggested practical implications: If your capacity to enjoy life experiences is higher at some ages

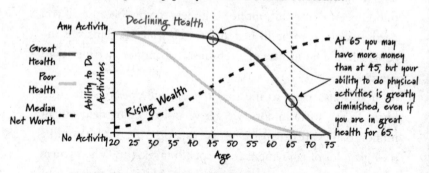

Ability to Enjoy Experiences Based on Health

Everyone's health declines with age. Wealth, on the other hand, tends to grow over the years as people save up more and more. But worsening health gradually constrains your enjoyment of that wealth as more and more physical activities become impossible to enjoy, no matter how much money you can afford to spend on them.

than others, then it makes sense to spend more of your money at certain ages than others! For example, because $100,000 has more value in your fifties than it does in your eighties, and your goal is to maximize your enjoyment of your money and your life, it's in your best interest to shift at least some of that money from your eighties into your fifties. For the same reason, it's in your best interest to shift some of it to your twenties, thirties, and forties, as well. Making these kinds of conscious financial shifts essentially creates a lifetime spending plan that takes into account the changing utility of money.

Whenever you shift in order to *spend* money, you are necessarily also shifting when you *save*. So, for example, instead of saving 20 percent of your income throughout your working years, some people would be better off saving almost nothing in their early twenties (as we've discussed), then gradually ramping up their saving rate during their late twenties and thirties as their income begins to rise. Then they should save even more than 20 percent in their forties—and then slow down their savings so that eventually (as I explain in the next chapter) they actually start outspending their earnings.

Notice that I am being careful to say that *some* people would be better off doing that. Everybody's situation is different. For example, some people's favorite activities, such as mere walking, are inexpensive; others don't require tip-top physical health. How much you should save also depends on how fast your income grows from year to year, where you live, and how fast your savings grow. Because of all these variables, and all the possible combinations they produce, there is no one-size-fits-all rule.

There you have it: It makes sense to spend more of your money at some ages than others, so it makes sense to adjust your balance of spending to saving over the years accordingly.

The Real Golden Years

We've all been told—like so many hardworking, diligent ants—that we need to save up our money for our "golden years" of retirement. But ironically, the real golden years—the period of maximum potential enjoyment because we have the most health and wealth—mostly come *before* the traditional retirement age of 65. And those real golden years are the years during which we should be doing most of our spending, not delaying gratification.

Too many people are making the mistake of investing in their future well past the point when those investments will ever pay off in ways that increase their overall lifetime fulfillment. Why do they persist? I think a lot of it is just the inertia (or, as I call it, autopilot) of doing what's worked in the past. Sometimes it's better to spend now, and other times you're better off saving up (and investing) your money for a potentially better experience in the future.

At the extremes, this is easy to see: Obviously, if you keep hoarding your money and don't spend any of it, your fulfillment curve will be minimal. And if you spend all your money now, you won't have any for the future. It's the Ant and the Grasshopper as I see the fable: There is a time to work (and save) and a time to play, and the optimal life requires planning for both survival and thriving. The grasshopper is so focused on thriving, on enjoying himself in the moment, that he forgets about survival and ends up living too short a life. But the ant is also making a big mistake: As a result of his hard work, he will live to see another year, but he is so preoccupied with survival that he doesn't get to enjoy summer and thrive. Neither extreme optimizes for lifetime fulfillment.

Understanding that moral is one thing, but putting it into practice is a different story. At any one point, it's not easy to know which way to go. The optimal balance between saving and spending is not obvious at all. If you've spent decades dutifully saving and investing your money, it can be hard to stop—assuming you're even aware that you should stop.

So what do you do? How do you achieve more balance in your life? I suggest several ways of thinking about the problem. Depending on who you are and how you think, different ones will resonate with you.

Balancing Health, Money, and Time Across Your Life

Think about the three basics people need to have to get the most out of life: health, free time, and money. The problem is that these things rarely all come together at once. Young people tend to have abundant health and a good deal of free time, but they don't usually have a lot of money. Retirees in their sixties, seventies, and beyond—the other end of the spectrum—have abundant time (and often more money than young people), but, unfortunately, they have less health, and thus a diminished ability to enjoy the time and money they do have than the young do.

What happens in between these two extremes? I think of this period as the real golden years because it usually includes a good combination of health and wealth. For example, a 35-year-old is still healthy enough to do most of the things a 25-year-old can do but typically earns a lot more. A 40-year-old (and, even more so, a 50-year-old) generally has slightly worse health than a 30-year-old but still has a pretty high degree of health—and, generally, a higher income than either the 25-year-old or the 35-year-old. So people in these middle years—neither very young nor very old—typically have a different problem: They face a time crunch, especially if they have children at home. This time crunch is their biggest obstacle to having positive life experiences. Not that children don't bring plenty of positive life experiences—they do—but between changing diapers, driving to various lessons and practices, and taking care of a larger household, there's just less time for other experiences. The same is true if you don't have children but find yourself working longer hours earning money than you did in your twenties.

To get the most positive life experiences at any age, you must balance your life, and this requires you to exchange an abundant resource in order to get more of a scarce one.

Every group already does this to some extent, though I believe they often get the magnitude wrong. Specifically, young

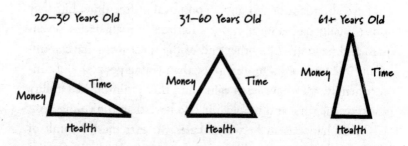

Shifting Balance of Health, Money, and Free Time

Each age tends to have a different balance of health, money, and free time. Because fulfillment requires reasonable amounts of all three, it's a good idea at every age to trade an abundance of one (such as money) to attain more of the other two (such as buying more health or free time).

people exchange their abundant time for money, sometimes to a fault—they should prize their free time more than most do. Old people spend a lot of their money trying to improve their health or to at least fight disease. People in the middle years sometimes trade money for time—and the more money they have, the more of it they should be using to buy time.

Most working people focus too much on getting more money. Let me explain why focusing on health and free time will yield more personal fulfillment.

Why Your Health Is More Valuable Than Your Money

Nothing has a greater effect on your ability to enjoy experiences —at any age—than your health. In fact, health is actually a lot more valuable than money, because no amount of money can ever make up for very poor health—whereas people in good health but with little money can still have many wonderful experiences.

And that's not just true in the extreme case of terrible health. Just being significantly overweight can put a damper on your enjoyment of life, if only because of all the extra pressure additional weight puts on your knees. I'll bet you know people who, because of bad knees or weak muscles or just self-consciousness about their bodies, avoid many experiences that others around them take pleasure in, such as hiking or ziplining or delighting in the water and the sun on the beach. Or they go on the hike with everyone else, but they're huffing and puffing, really struggling to eke out any kind of enjoyment out of this potentially fun activity. Some of these people might even have been athletes when they were younger; it's just that when they stopped being physically active, they continued to pile on the calories until they were 30 or 50 pounds overweight. It's easy for that to happen, especially for people with jobs that consume most of their waking hours and energy and require sitting in front of a computer screen all day. And to what end? When the demanding job finally brings you financial success, do you still have the key ingredient (health) for enjoying that success?

Healthcare providers understand this problem better than most of us, just because of the many suffering patients they see. But even people working in healthcare aren't immune to neglecting their own health. Let me give you just one example, this one with a happy ending. Stephen Stern, a chiropractor in Massachusetts who went public with his own decades-long struggles with weight, had been treating aching patients for decades and yet allowed his weight to yo-yo. He'd take up exercise and lose some weight, but then he'd stop exercising and gain all the weight right back, losing whatever physical fitness he had worked hard to achieve.

When Stern was 59, he finally realized he couldn't let this pattern continue—not if he wanted to avoid the fate of his less fortunate patients. As an article about him put it, "he'd seen patients his age and younger who'd lost the ability to do things they loved —not just through injury or illness, but often through simple neglect of their bodies. He knew that when people at this stage of life lost physical capabilities, often they never got them back."

So Stern was determined to become fit again before he turned 60. This time he took a more gradual path to fitness than he had in the past; his body could no longer take the intense training regimens he'd put himself through in his younger years, but he could still regain a great deal of fitness through walking and calisthenics. And this slow but steady approach worked: His old knee pains disappeared, and by age 66 he found that he could perform impressive feats of strength and balance, like a bent-knees handstand. His efforts at improving his fitness paid off in renewed confidence and competence—and in joyous experiences he wouldn't otherwise have, like summiting mountains with his daughter. Though he can now do things most 30-year-olds cannot, he knows he's never going to be as fit as a fit 30-year-old. What he's actually accomplished is peak health for his age. "I'm an older man and I move the way an older man can move!"

Stories like Stephen Stern's are inspiring—we all want to hear that it's never too late. But that's not why I'm telling you the story. The reality is that sometimes it really is too late to reverse decades of neglect and abuse, something Stern understood. And even when it's not too late, it's always better to have started investing in your health earlier. What I'm really trying to get across is that improved health improves everything in your life, makes every experience more enjoyable, at every age.

In our three-pronged model—where fulfillment from a single experience is a function of health, money, and free time—health is the single biggest factor (or multiplier) affecting the size of a person's lifetime fulfillment curve: Our simulations show that even a small permanent reduction in health at some point in a person's life amounts to a large reduction in the person's lifetime fulfillment score.

Why would that be—why does health affect lifetime fulfillment more than either free time or money? When adjusting the health input, we are adjusting the rate at which your body will decline. How fast your body's health declines depends on how in shape (or not) you are now. So if you are 2 percent from optimal health now, you may be 20 percent from optimal health 10 or 15 years from now. Basically, there is a compounding effect to being in poor health. I don't claim to be a doctor, but here is an example of how I see it working, and how it impacts your enjoyment of activities.

Let's say you are 10 pounds overweight. That doesn't seem so bad at first, but each pound of excess weight means four extra pounds of force on your knees. Ten pounds of excess weight is equivalent to 40 pounds of excess force your knees were not designed to handle. Naturally, over time, the cartilage in your knees will deteriorate and tear, and perhaps your bones will start to rub against each other. Your natural shock absorbers have been worn out, making it painful for you to walk for any extended period, and running is pretty much unbearable. This leads to more weight gain and other associated problems. It's no wonder that knee replacement surgery is one of the fastest-growing surgeries in the USA, closely tracking the rise in obesity. In any case, that seemingly inconsequential ten pounds ballooned via compounding into other serious health problems and a lack of enjoyment of activities associated with walking.

As I've stated before, movement is life, and your experiences will be greatly diminished when your movement becomes painful or limited. There are many paths of decay until we ultimately die. We all wish to have the greatest physical function until we die, yet many of us will have greater exponential decay at an earlier time in our lives—resulting in lower ability and lower enjoyment—as a result of how we have treated our bodies. Einstein supposedly called compound interest the greatest force in the universe. Small changes in health can lead to a *negative* compounding that has enormous impacts on your lifetime fulfillment and experience points.

The good news from all this: If you take even small steps to improve your health now (improving even 1 percent and avoiding the negative compounding effects), you will have vastly increased your total experience points.

There's a clear implication in this observation, and it's one you've doubtless heard before: People of all ages should be spending more time and money on their health. No age group spends more on health than the elderly, whose healthcare spending aims to treat degenerative diseases, manage pain, and prolong life. But earlier investments in health would actually yield greater lifetime fulfillment. Preventive steps like eating right and strengthening muscles helps you keep your health as high as possible for as long as possible—and makes every experience more enjoyable. I'm not just talking about being able to ski into your seventies instead of having to settle for shuffleboard, or playing tennis instead of pickleball. No, even simple, everyday activities like walking up and down stairs, getting up out of a chair, or carrying bags of groceries become easier and more pleasant when you're physically fit and not carrying around excess body weight on weak bones and muscles. Just think: How quickly you get tired on a day of sightseeing, snowboarding, or playing with little kids will have an obvious impact on how much enjoyment you get out of that day. Now multiply that out to all your future potential days of such experiences!

This is why I love making prop bets tied to health goals—the kind where I'll bet a ridiculous amount of money that a buddy won't manage to run a marathon or won't be able to lose a certain amount of weight. I've made more of these kinds of bets than I can count, and I think they're great, because the value of attaining a big, life-changing health goal far exceeds the money at stake. A recent favorite (despite the fact that I lost the bet) involved two young guys I know from the poker world, brothers Jaime and Matt Staples. At the start of the bet, Jaime was obese, and had made no secret of his past attempts at weight loss —whereas Matt was a bit underweight, and he wanted to build muscle. To motivate them both to move toward their goals, I placed a single bet: The pair would get a large sum from me if, in exactly one year, they reached the same weight (technically, within one pound of each other).

Amazingly, their transformation was tremendous: Jaime's weight went down by more than 100 pounds, while Matt gained more than 50, much of it muscle. You can see the before-and-after pictures on the Internet. Obviously, they were happy to win and were proud of their accomplishment—but even if they had lost the bet after getting close, the monetary loss (only one-fiftieth of my stake, since we'd set the odds at 50–1) would have been worth the benefits of improved health, especially given their young age. They will have many years to enjoy the heightened fulfillment they get from having attained these health goals. Better health doesn't just give you a better retirement years from now—investing in your health is investing in every single subsequent experience!

Don't Undersell Your Time

The other big opportunity I see for creating a more balanced life is to exchange money for free time—a tactic that usually has the most impact in one's middle years, when you have more money than time. The classic example is laundry, a time-consuming weekly chore that most people dread doing and that, in many places, can be done inexpensively by an outside service that specializes in it.

Let me clarify. Suppose your work nets you $40 per hour, and suppose laundry takes you two hours each week, because you're slow and inefficient at this chore. A professional service that has better equipment and does laundry all day every day is much more efficient than you are and can turn a profit even while charging you $50 or less. Is it worth it to spend $50 per week on a service that picks up a week's worth of your dirty laundry and delivers it clean and neatly folded the following week? Absolutely, because at $40 per hour, two hours of your time is worth $80. This is true even when you are not using that time to earn money; you can be using the time to take your kids to the park, or to read a book, or to meet a friend for lunch, or whatever you would enjoy more than doing the laundry.

Laundry is just one example; the same logic applies to any undesirable chore, like housecleaning. To me this kind of out-sourcing always seemed like a no-brainer—so much so that I started doing it in my twenties, when I had a much lower in-come. Even then, I would choose to spend a Saturday morning rollerblading in Central Park and going to brunch at Sarabeth's rather than cleaning my apartment. And thank the Lord that I chose to spend that money—because I now have lifelong mem-ories of many pleasant weekends.

The more money you have, the more you should be using this tactic, because your time is a lot more scarce and finite than your cash. I am constantly trading money back into time. I'll never get more than 24 hours in a day, but I can do my utmost to free up as much of that finite time as I possibly can.

This isn't just my personal experience or economic theoriz-ing. Research in psychology backs me up: People who spend money on time-saving purchases experience greater life satisfac-tion, regardless of their income. In other words, you don't have to be rich to enjoy the benefits of spending money to free up time.

By running a field experiment in which they gave some working adults money to spend on a time-saving purchase (while giving another group of working adults the same amount of money to spend on a material purchase), researchers could begin to explain why people who spend money to save time are happier: Using time-saving services reduced time pressure, they found, and reduced time pressure improved the day's mood. If done repeatedly, such daily mood lifts improve overall life satisfaction.

That makes sense to me, but I also think that something more than the relief of time pressure is at work. Here's how I see it: If you pay to get out of doing tasks you don't enjoy, you are simultaneously reducing the number of negative life experiences and increasing the number of positive life experiences (for which you now have more time). How can that *not* make you happier with your life?

You might realize with some regret that you got the balance wrong—for example, let's say that you're now 35 or 40, and in your twenties you spent all your time making money and therefore missed out on lots of great experiences. Although you'll never get those years back, you can try to rebalance your life now. Therefore, you need to really focus on having more experiences now, while you still have a high degree of health, and spending more than a person your age who *didn't* trade all that time for money. For every moment, there is an ideal experience to be having in that moment.

Your Personal Interest Rate

You know how I've proposed that your ability to extract enjoyment from money declines with age? Well, the corollary to that is that the older you are, the more someone should have to pay you to delay an experience. How much they should pay you is what I call your *personal interest rate*—which rises with your age. This idea immediately hits home for people in finance, who are used to thinking about interest rates and the time value of money. Let me explain.

Suppose you're 20 years old; at this age, you can afford to wait a year or two to have an experience, because you can typically have the same experience later. Therefore, your personal interest is low—someone doesn't have to pay you much for you to be willing to delay the experience. Let's say you wanted to take a trip to Mexico this summer, but your boss said to you, "I could really use you here this summer. I know you wanted to take this Mexico trip, but would you consider taking it next summer instead? I would pay you x percent of the price of the trip to do that." Okay, interesting offer. So how high would x have to be for you to agree? 10 percent? 25 percent?

Now suppose you're 80. At this point, delaying an experience becomes much more costly, so your x would have to be much higher than when you were 20. Even if someone paid you 50 percent of the price of the trip to delay it, you should *not* necessarily take the offer—your personal interest rate at age 80 may be higher than 50 percent. It might even be higher than 100 percent.

What happens if you are terminally ill? Once you know that you won't be around a year from now, your personal interest rate is off the charts—there is no amount of money someone can pay you to delay a valuable experience.

So your personal interest rate rises with age, but unfortunately we don't always act as if it does. If this concept of a personal interest rate works for you, though, then keeping it in mind when you are considering buying an experience can help you decide whether it's worth it to spend the money now or to save it for another time.

Would You Rather?

If the personal interest rate doesn't do it for you, you can think in terms of simple multiples of an experience. This is how the famous marshmallow test, created for preschoolers by psychologist Walter Mischel at Stanford in the 1960s, is set up: Would you rather have one marshmallow now, or two marshmallows 15 minutes from now? Many three-year-olds might say they'd rather have two marshmallows in 15 minutes, but once that tempting marshmallow is in front of them, many can't wait. Adults usually have a better ability to delay gratification—very often to the point where delaying gratification no longer serves them well. In effect, they are opting not for one marshmallow now or two marshmallows in 15 minutes, but for one and a half marshmallows ten years later!

When it's presented in that way, the mistake seems obvious. So how do you apply this logic to your spending decisions? When you face a choice, such as whether to go on a trip on your next vacation or to save your money for later, ask yourself, *Would I rather have one trip now, or two such trips* x *years from now?* Here's how to figure out what *x* is. Whenever you have some discretionary income—whether it's $10 or $100 or $1,000 or more—you have a choice. You can spend the money now or you can save it for later. If you save it for later, there's potential for the money to grow, because unless you're putting it under your mattress, you're investing it in something (like the stock market) that promises a return above the rate of inflation. This inflation-adjusted interest rate is called the "real interest."

The longer you let the investment grow, the more money you end up with—so after a number of years, your principal ($100, for example) could double (to $200) or even triple (to $300). The real interest rate varies, but let's take the example of 8 percent annual growth. (That is a little more than the average stock market return since its inception—again, after adjusting for inflation.) At that rate, your $100 becomes $147 in five years. In ten years, it becomes $216—more than enough to buy two of whatever experience you thought about buying now.

The question is: Should you wait nine to ten years to get two of the experiences you could have today? It's totally up to you, and your answer will depend a lot on the kind of experience it is—as it should. For you to even consider the choice of one now versus two or more later, the experience has to be one that can be replicated. (Once-in-a-lifetime events like weddings and graduations of family and best friends obviously can't.) You should also think about whether the experience might actually be better if you delay it: Sometimes by waiting, you can use the extra money to buy a significantly better version of the same experience. I can tell you, for example, that experiencing Las Vegas at 40 is much better than Las Vegas at 20, assuming you have significantly more money at 40 than at 20. It's like two different Las Vegases. I'm not saying that no 20-year-old should go to Las Vegas. My point is there are times to delay gratification, because doing so will net you more life experience points.

So it depends on the experience you're trying to have. But in general, I think you'll find that if you ask yourself, *Would I rather?* you will naturally choose to delay when you're younger and to avoid delays when you are older. If you're 20, your answer will probably be that you're willing to wait. Why? Because ten years on, you'll probably still have much of your current health, and two trips are better than one. But if you're 70, you probably don't want to wait until you're 80! Your declining health—which means that the experience might not be available to you if you delay having it—tells you to have the experience now.

So you see, thinking in terms of *Would I rather?* is really getting at the same issue as the personal interest rate: The older you get, the less willing you should be to delay an experience, even if someone pays you a lot of money to do so.

Solving for Maximum Fulfillment: Introducing the Die with Zero App

Throughout this chapter I've been talking about balancing the spending and saving you do throughout your life. I've already explained in general terms that you should shift spending to more or less the right ages. And you understand the three factors that most affect your ability to enjoy your life energy: health, free time, and money. But if your goal is to *maximize* lifetime enjoyment, that means finding out how much to spend each year, a number that varies depending on each person's circumstances.

To find that number, I needed a computer program that takes in each person's individual circumstances and runs a bunch of calculations to determine the optimal spending plan for that person. I'm happy to say that, with help from an economist, I've developed this app. Now, using this app isn't necessary for getting more out of your life energy; you'll be able to do that just by following the advice throughout this book. But if you want to be even more optimal—if you want to squeeze out every available bit of your life energy—the app can help. To find out more about the app and how it can help, please check out the appendix.

Recommendations

- Think about your current physical health: What life experiences can you have now that you might not be able to have later?
- Think of one way in which you can invest your time or your money to improve your health and thereby improve all of your future life experiences.
- Learn about how to improve your eating habits to improve your health. Of the many books on this subject, the one I know well and always recommend is *Eat to Live,* by Joel Fuhrman, M.D.
- Do more of the physical activities that you already enjoy (such as dancing or hiking) that will also improve your enjoyment of future experiences.
- If your ability to enjoy experiences is more constrained by time than by money or by health, think of one or two ways you can spend some money now to free up more of your time.

7

START TO TIME-BUCKET YOUR LIFE

Rule No. 7:
Think of your life as
distinct seasons.

When my daughters were little, we loved watching *Pooh's Heffalump Movie* together. I think it's the most wonderful kids' movie there is—a sweet, innocent story about friendship. We watched it many times. But then one day, when my younger daughter was ten, I suggested we watch the Heffalump movie and, to my astonishment, she just wasn't interested anymore. All of a sudden, she thought she was too old for it!

If someone had told me that by this date my kid would stop wanting to watch the Heffalump movie, I probably would have watched it with her a lot more. Unfortunately, in real life you rarely get an exact date for when you will no longer be able to do something—these things just seem to fade away. And until they're gone, you don't give their gradual demise much thought, if any. You just kind of assume that some things will last forever. But of course, they don't. That's sad, granted, but there's good news: Just realizing that they don't last forever, that everything eventually fades and dies, can make you appreciate everything more in the here and now.

This entire book is predicated on the hard, cold truth that we will all die and, as we age, our health will gradually decline. But there's another, less obvious truth about "dying" that has important implications for how you should live your life: We all die a multitude of deaths throughout our lives. (I'll explain that shortly.) This chapter explores the practical implications of this universal process, of passing from one stage in your life to the next. In addition, this chapter gives you a tool—known as time bucketing—for planning your life experiences accordingly.

No Clear End Points

My experience with the Heffalump movie is just one example. For several years, I was living the life of a dad who watches his favorite kids' movie surrounded by his young children. But then one day that stage of my life and theirs was gone. I'm still here, of course, and I can still enjoy other experiences with my daughters—watching their soccer games and dance recitals, for example, and taking them on trips. But someday they will grow up and that version of me will disappear, too.

Likewise, but for reasons of my own inevitable aging, there will eventually be a last time I ever go wave-running, and a last time I play in a poker tournament, and a last time I'll be able to board a plane and fly somewhere exotic. Some of these final experiences will come sooner than others, but all will definitely come at some point in the (hopefully) far distant future.

Now, I'm not trying to be morbid, nor am I trying to present so much in the way of gloom and doom. My point—and this is important—is that the day I die and the day I stop being able to enjoy certain experiences are two distinctly different dates. And this is true for everyone.

That is what I mean when I say that we die many deaths in the course of our lives: The teenager in you dies, the college student in you dies, the single unattached you dies, the version of you that's a parent of an infant dies, and so on. Once each of these mini-deaths occurs, there's no going back. Maybe "dies" is a bit harsh, but you get the idea: We all keep moving forward, progressing from one stage or phase of our lives to the next. So much death and doom, I know—but the upside is that we have many lives to live and to enjoy and to maximize!

The challenge of maximizing these lives is not just that there's no going back. Think back to your own past experiences. When was the very last time you went outside and played with your childhood friends? When was the very last time you talked to a beloved professor before he or she died? Even if you can recall the exact date, you probably didn't know it in advance. Unlike school years and round-trip vacations, the end points of most periods in our lives come and go without much fanfare. The periods may overlap, but sooner or later each one comes to an end.

Because of this eventual finality of all of life's passing phases, you can delay some experiences for only so long before the window of opportunity on these experiences shuts forever. The best analogy I can think of is a set of different swimming pools, the kind some large resorts have—there's usually a wading pool for little kids, a pool with a waterslide for older kids and teens, an adults-only pool, maybe even a pool for lap swimming and a pool just for seniors. Now, you can go in every pool for as long as you want, but only if you follow that pool's precise rules.

So if you don't learn to swim by the time you're too old for the kiddie pool, you can still go to the teen pool, and later to the adult pool; but if you're no longer a teen, no more waterslide for you! It doesn't matter how strong a swimmer you are or how much you regret your fear of the waterslide when you were younger. Likewise, in real life, you can safely delay some experiences for a future period—if you don't take certain trips or pursue certain physical activities in your twenties, you might still be able to take them in your thirties—but this ability to transfer physical experiences from one time period to another is limited. In fact, it's actually more limited than most people seem to realize when they delay and delay. Some people act as if they will have access to the kiddie pool and the teen pool all their lives—or that their whole life is one big pool that they can use at any time. But then time passes and they find themselves in the senior pool and ask themselves how they wound up there!

Regret-Free Living

Do you see what I'm saying? The problem of confronting overly delayed gratification and the resulting regret doesn't occur just once, at the end of one's life. Rather, it can occur at *every* period during your life, from the bookworm teenager who missed out on all the fun of high school by making too many sacrifices for the sake of a supposedly brighter future to the middle-aged dad who repeatedly skipped irreplaceable experiences with his own teens by constantly hustling for one job promotion after another. Sometimes people realize their mistake just before the window of opportunity closes—like when one's children are getting ready to leave the nest—and sometimes the recognition comes when it's too late to do anything at all about it except resolve to do better in their next life stage.

The saddest, though, is when the realization doesn't hit until you're facing your own mortality, when it really is too late to change anything and all you can do is make peace with your past.

For those of us who still have time to make changes and adjustments, it can be enlightening and even motivating to read or hear about other people's deathbed regrets.

Many of these are particular to each individual, of course, but if you listen to dozens of stories about people's deathbed regrets, common patterns do tend to emerge. An Australian woman named Bronnie Ware, whose work as a palliative caregiver put her at the bedsides of patients with just weeks left to live, talked with her patients about what they wished they had done differently in their lives, and found five key regrets coming up more often than any others. As she describes in a popular online article and in a subsequent book, the two most common regrets are ones that are most relevant to my message.

Her patients' number one regret was wishing they'd had the courage to live a life true to themselves—as opposed to the life that others expected of them. It's a regret about not pursuing your dreams, and therefore having those dreams go unfulfilled. If you ignore what you truly value in life and instead pursue a path that the rest of your surrounding everyday culture foists upon you, you risk having real regret at the end of your days. In

American culture, which so often values hard work and earning money to the exclusion of other important values (such as leisure, adventure, and relationships), it stands to reason that people often come to the end of their days really wishing they hadn't made this kind of sacrifice. As the old saying goes, "No one ever regrets not having spent more time in the office."

Along those lines, the second regret—and actually the top regret among Ware's male patients—was this: "I wish I had not worked so hard." That hits right at the heart of what I'm preaching. "All of the men I nursed deeply regretted spending so much of their lives on the treadmill of a work existence," Ware writes. Women had this regret, too, but, as Ware points out, her patients were from an older generation, when fewer women worked outside the home. And when people say they regret working so hard, they are not talking about the hard work of raising children; they are talking about working to make a living to pay the bills and, as a result, missing "their children's youth and their partner's companionship."

Now, let's take a deep breath. I recognize that all this talk about death and regrets in life sounds very depressing. I realize that by attempting to raise awareness of what you will eventually lose forever, I am handing you a kind of anticipatory grief. But believe it or not, thinking about impending loss can actually make you happier. A most revealing experiment with college freshmen shows why.

A team of psychologists asked one group of young students to imagine that they would be moving far away in 30 days, and told them to plan their next 30 days accordingly: It would be the students' last chance for a very long time to enjoy all the special people and places they'd come to like about their college. In short, the students were urged to savor their remaining time on campus. Then, every week that month, the researchers asked the students to write down their activities.

By contrast, another group of freshmen weren't told to imagine anything or to do any kind of savoring of their days—they merely had to track their daily activities. Guess what happened? As you can imagine, the students in the first group were happier by the end of the 30 days than the second group. Whether they did more or just managed to squeeze more enjoyment out of whatever they did on a daily basis, the mere act of deliberately thinking about their time as limited definitely helped.

What's the takeaway here? Being aware that your time is limited can clearly motivate you to make the most of the time you do have.

We've all experienced some version of this effect when going on vacation in a new place. As tourists, we know all too well that we have only a week or however long at our destination—so we plan ahead to make sure we pack in as many landmarks, tours, activities, and other experiences unique to the place we're visiting as we can. If we're visiting friends, we make sure to spend plenty of time with those folks, and we try to savor every moment. In other words, we make a full and conscious effort to treat our time as the scarce resource that it is.

Now, that's usually very different from what we do when we're back home, where we're much more likely to take our hometown's everyday, routine attractions for granted. It's not just that we're busy with other pressing, daily responsibilities, even though it is true that we are and it would be unrealistic to live your life as if you were always on vacation. But it's more than that—it's also that most people just have the sense that there's no time urgency near home; they act as if they will always be able to visit that museum or that nearby beach or that friend some other time. As a result, we spend many of our evenings watching TV, and we fritter away our weekends. In short, when something feels abundant and endless, the truth is, we don't always value it. But the reality, of course, is that the time you get to spend in each phase in your life is *not* that abundant, and it's certainly not unlimited.

Unlike some other topics in this book, the idea of having a finite number of phases with a finite number of days in each has nothing to do with money. Yes, the specific experiences you can have in each time period *do* have to do with money, but the reality and implications of these finite periods do not. Every person says things like "I've always wanted to hike such-and-such trail" or "I've always wanted to take my kids to such-and-such place." Experiences like that exist on every budget. Let me suggest a simple tool to raise awareness of these phases in your life, in order to help you plan the experiences you want to have during your lifetime, and therefore to help you avoid excessive delays.

Learn from Your "Time Buckets"

Time buckets are a simple tool for discovering what you want your life to look like in broad strokes. Here's what I suggest you do. Draw a timeline of your life from now to the grave, then divide it into intervals of five or ten years. Each of those intervals —say, from age 30 to 40, or from 70 to 75—is a time bucket, which is just a random grouping of years.

Then think about what key experiences—activities or events —you definitely want to have during your lifetime. We all have dreams in life, but I have found that it's extremely helpful to actually *write them all down in a list*. It doesn't have to be a complete list; in fact, you can't know right now everything you'll ever want to do, because, as you know, new experiences and new people you meet tend to reveal unexpected additional interests that you'll want to pursue. Life is all about discovery. And you will revisit this list later in life, too.

But I'm sure you already have some ideas about which experiences you'd want to have at some point, some perhaps more than once. For example, you might want to have a child, run the Boston Marathon, hike the Himalayas, build a house, file a patent, start a business, volunteer for Doctors Without Borders, dine at a Michelin-star restaurant, attend the Sundance Film Festival, go skiing 50 times, go to the opera, take a cruise to Alaska, read 20 classic novels, attend the Super Bowl, compete in a Scrabble tournament, visit Yellowstone, see autumn in Vermont, take your kids to Disneyland three times, and so on. You get the idea. Be as creative as you want.

Your list will be your own unique expression of who you are, because your life experiences are what make you who you are. Key point: As you're making your list, don't worry about money; money at this point is just a distraction from the overall goal, which is to envision what you *want* your life to be like.

Then, once you have your list of items, start to drop each of your hoped-for pursuits into the specific buckets, based on when you'd ideally have each experience. For example, if you want to go skiing 50 times in your life, during which decades or five-year buckets would you like to have those ski days? Here, too, don't think about money just yet—rather, think about the point in your life when you'd really like to have each experience.

Some of these bucketing decisions will be easier than others. In fact, you probably already have a decent idea of some of the wonderful experiences you'd like to enjoy in your lifetime.

Filling Your Time Buckets

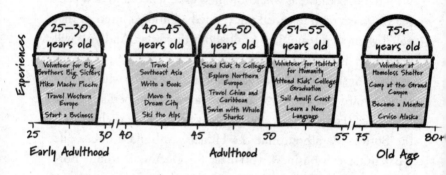

As you time-bucket your life, you parcel out a single list of experiences into different and distinct time sections of your life.

As for your other "wish list" items, well, for example, you can always travel to a faraway place. But as we've noted, it's always easier to travel when you're in your forties or fifties than when you're in your seventies or eighties. The point is, today's the day to start actively and consciously thinking and planning for your years ahead.

In general, using the time-buckets approach will make you begin to realize that some experiences are better done at certain ages. Mountain climbing and attending loud concerts, for example, are much more fun when you're younger. Not surprisingly, the most physically demanding activities tend to fall on the left (younger) side of the timeline. You probably won't be skiing much at 80. Yes, some people run the Boston Marathon in their seventies, and one exceptionally fit woman named Katherine Beiers completed the race when she was 85. But these individuals, of course, are outliers. And even for Beiers, the marathon at 85 was not her first—but her 14th.

A Season for Everything: Time Buckets vs. a Bucket List

As you go through this bucket exercise, you'll come to see for yourself that there's a season for everything. That being said, you might begin to sense that some desired experiences conflict with other experiences. Or you might realize that some of the activities you want to do won't happen at all unless you begin to plan for them now.

And just to clarify: This list is the opposite of the so-called bucket list, which is typically a single accounting of all the things you hope to do before you "kick the bucket," so to speak. The more traditional bucket list is usually put together by an older individual who, when confronted with their mortality, begins to scratch out a list of activities and pursuits they not only haven't done yet but now feel compelled to do quickly, before time runs out.

By contrast, by dividing goals into time buckets, you are taking a much more proactive approach to your life. In effect, you're looking ahead over several coming decades of your life and trying to plan out all the various activities, events, and experiences you'd like to have. Time buckets are proactive and let you plan your life; a bucket list, on the other hand, is a much more reactive effort in a sudden race against time.

Now, you might notice as you fill up your time buckets that some experiences are more flexible than others. For example, you can still enjoy visiting libraries, watching classic movies, reading novels, and playing chess well into your old age. Taking a cruise can be enjoyable at just about any age.

Still, as you start filling up your time buckets, you'll probably see that the experiences you want to have in life don't fall evenly across the ages. Instead, they naturally cluster during certain periods—taking on roughly the shape of the right side of a bell curve (see figure below).

As long as you're still ignoring the money factor, and still focusing primarily on your health and your free time, that bell will probably skew to the left—because you'll want to have most of your experiences (especially those with physically demanding activities) when you're at peak health to enjoy them, and before you're constrained by the demands of parenthood. If your life plan includes children, the experiences you want to have with them will cluster a little later, probably creating a peak around your thirties and forties. Again, all that's true even if you don't take the cost of experiences into consideration.

Okay. Remember, we've been focusing only on two key com-

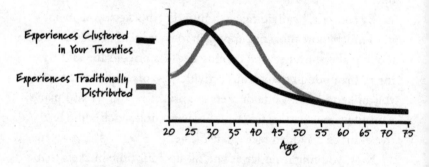

Experiences Clustered in Your Twenties vs More Traditionally Distributed Around Midlife

Experiences Clustered in Your Twenties

Experiences Traditionally Distributed

Age

Without the constraint of money, most of your experiences would optimally occur in your twenties and thirties, when your health is highest. But in reality, most people's spending is clustered around midlife instead.

ponents of your time buckets: your physical health and your life's dreams. We deliberately pushed financial concerns off to the side, because it's always too easy to blow off our dreams by simply saying, "Sounds really nice, but let's face it . . . I can't afford that." Focusing on money distracts from the hard truth that time and health are fleeting.

But financial concerns are real, so read on to the next chapter, where we'll talk about how to make sure you don't miss the opportunity to spend your money while you still have time on your side.

Recommendations

- If time-bucketing your whole life feels a bit overwhelming, just do the exercise with three time buckets covering the next 30 years. Know you can always add more to your list; just do it long before your age and health become a real factor.
- If you have children, think about your own version of the Heffalump movie: What one experience do you want to have more of with them in the next year or two, before that phase of their life and your life is over?

8

——

KNOW YOUR PEAK

Rule No. 8:
Know when to stop
growing your wealth.

I recently celebrated my 50th birthday. I certainly had a wonderful time on that day, but it actually wasn't the biggest party of my life. My biggest, best party happened five years earlier, after I had set out to plan the most memorable 45th birthday celebration I could afford. The idea was to bring together all of my family and friends from every stage of my life and to introduce them all to one of my favorite places on the planet: the serene and beautiful Caribbean island of St. Barts, where my wife and I had spent our honeymoon.

Even though turning 45 is just a semi-milestone, I knew I

didn't want to wait until I turned 50 to have this experience: My mom was already old, and I wanted her to be able to fly in and to fully enjoy the celebration. (My dad was already debilitated and couldn't travel, so it was even more important that my mom attend.) Plus my friends weren't getting any younger, either! Who knew if there'd ever be another chance to bring all of these people together? That year was the right time bucket, and I was determined to make the party happen. I wanted to have this significant and unique memory for the rest of my life.

Of course, this was going to cost some money. Fortunately, by this point in my life, through a bit of skill and a tremendous amount of luck in my work as an energy trader, I was doing well financially. But I know money is a concern for everyone, and many of the people I wanted to invite, including friends from childhood and college, couldn't afford to fly to St. Barts and pay for a room in the secluded hotel I had my eye on. The people you share experiences with truly affect the quality of the experience—and nowhere is that more true than at a once-in-a-lifetime event. So I knew that if I wanted to have this kind of unique birthday bash, I was going to have to step up and pay for a lot of my guests to attend.

Still, my wealth is finite, just like everybody else's, and as I started running the numbers, I ran up against my limits. Having this dream celebration would cost a big portion of my liquid net worth. Was it really a good idea to spend that much money on just one week, no matter how amazing that week might turn out to be?

We all face some version of this question whenever we consider a major purchase. Of course, the dollar amounts differ from person to person, often by orders of magnitude, but the core question is the same for all of us: What's the best way to spend our money for maximum enjoyment and in order to generate maximum memories?

Now, you already know some of my answers to this question: Invest in experiences that yield long-lasting memories, always bear in mind that everyone's health declines with age, give your money to your children before you die instead of saving for their inheritance, and learn to balance current enjoyment with later gratification. But even though I'm a big believer in these principles, my 45th birthday party gave me pause: I had to talk myself over the psychological hurdle of spending a fortune on a single, weeklong party, no matter how memorable it would be. I had to tell myself again and again that I was never going to turn 45 again and asked myself when—short of my funeral, someday way in the future—I was ever going to be able to get all these key people in my life together again. Once I got over that psychological hurdle, though, I was all in, and I went all out, creating the best party my money could buy.

The Party of a Lifetime

I rented out the secluded beachfront Hotel Taïwana, on the white sandy beach of the island's largest bay—all 22 rooms and suites. To house everyone, I also booked several rooms at the equally stunning hotel next door, the Cheval Blanc. I bought flights for dozens of guests. On top of all that, I arranged for boat trips and picnics and nightly food and entertainment: One evening was sushi-and-karaoke night, another was a night of old-school R&B.

Then there was Natalie Merchant. When I was living in New York in my twenties, just starting out and sharing a tiny apartment with a roommate, he and I used to listen to *Tigerlily,* Merchant's 1995 debut solo album. I loved that album. And I knew that the former 10,000 Maniacs singer's mellow lyrical style would set the perfect mood for one special evening and that it would be a hit with everyone from my mom to the guys I'd grown up with in Jersey City. So I arranged through Merchant's reps to bring her down to the island for a private concert, telling my guests only that we'd have a surprise guest.

The night of the private concert was as wonderful as you can imagine. I remember holding my wife from behind and just listening to the music and to Merchant telling the story of how she had composed one of the songs, and I also remember drinking champagne like crazy. It was a pleasure seeing my mom chatting with the great singer, too. But it wasn't just that concert that was incredible—I would never change anything about that trip.

Picture it: You're walking down from your room to the beautiful beach on a crystal-clear day, with gentle waves rolling in, and wherever you look, all you see are your loved ones. You see your best friend from college, and then you walk some more and you glimpse your best friend from your working years. Your mom is coming out of her cabana. You see other close friends on their deck or by the pool, and everyone is in awe of the beauty all around. And everyone is happy! Trust me, sharing that common experience is just the best feeling ever. At some point I actually had the thought *This might just be what heaven looks like.* That feeling came to me again and again. The whole week was awesome in every way and I'll never forget it, not until my brain stops working.

To this day, the people in my life are still talking about that week, and every so often some little thing happens that reminds me of that wonderful party—and all those glorious feelings come rushing back again. Reliving those days and nights in my mind feels almost as good as actually being there. At the end of my life, I am convinced, my joy will come from my memories —and that trip to St. Barts will be right near the top of the list.

That's why I have absolutely no regrets about the insane amount of money I spent on that one week—nor the fact that I didn't wait until my 50th birthday to have the party of a lifetime. In fact, by the time my 50th rolled around, my dad had died, and my mom's health had, unfortunately, declined substantially. My brother and two sisters were there, but some of my friends couldn't make it this time. From my perspective, it had been a very good decision to splurge on that extraordinary gathering five years earlier.

Or . . . I could have not splurged on that lavish party when I was 45. Instead I could have celebrated my birthday by just looking at my monthly investment savings and IRA statements. But what kind of memory would that be?

Look, many of us are inclined to delay gratification and save for the future. And the *ability* to delay gratification serves us well. Being able to get to work on time, paying everyday bills, taking care of our kids, putting food on the table—these are the essentials in life. But actually delaying gratification is helpful only to a point. If you have your nose to the grindstone too much every day, you run the risk of waking up one morning and realizing that you may have delayed *too* much. And, at the extreme, indefinitely delayed gratification means *no* gratification. So at what point is it better not to delay?

Well, there are a couple of ways to answer that question. One is *year to year*, as chapter 6, "Balance Your Life," showed: Throughout your life you have to balance your spending on the present with your saving for the future. The optimal balance shifts from year to year because your health and income are likely to change each year.

The other way to answer the question of optimal balance is by looking at your lifetime savings as a whole, and how to do that is the focus of this chapter. Now, this is not how most people think about spending and saving, so let me explain what I mean.

First of all, think about everything you own right now, from your house to your baseball card collection, from the value of your investments in the stock market to the cash in your wallet. These are your total assets. If you have any debt, such as student loans, a mortgage, or car loans, then total up all those loans and subtract that amount from your total assets. What you're left with is your *net worth*: what you *own* minus what you *owe*. Sounds familiar, right? Net worth is a basic concept, and it's one we touched on earlier when we looked at data showing that Americans' median net worth tends to rise with age. If you understood that discussion, you already understand the next important point, which is that a person's net worth isn't the same throughout their life.

That's a key point to understanding the peak: your net worth tends to change over your lifetime. That's just how it is for most people. For a good chunk of your life, especially when you are starting out, you are simply spending the money that you are currently earning. At that early stage of your life, you are not increasing your net worth: If you're living in a rented apartment, carrying a lot of student loan debt, and not yet earning enough to pay off that debt, you have a negative net worth, because you owe more than you own.

But as you chip away at those student loans—and assuming your income rises faster than your spending—you typically start to save money, which means your net worth can start to grow from negative to positive. And it becomes more and more positive over time: If you stay gainfully employed, your net worth generally keeps rising, regardless of whether the rise is slow or fast. I'm not saying that's how it *should* be—that's just how it usually is. Let's say your net worth at age 25 is $2,000, and then your net worth at age 30 is $10,000. By age 35 it will most likely be some number higher than $10,000—and it will typically be higher than that at 40, and higher still at 45. The statistics on household net worth (by age of head of household) bear out this trend.

Or look at the rates of homeownership, since owning your own home is a common way to build wealth. (You might not think of your home in the same way as you do about money in the bank, but there's no denying that owning a house adds to your net worth.) Whereas only about 35 percent of Americans under 35 own their own place, the homeownership rate for Americans aged 35–44 is nearly 60 percent, and it is nearly 70 percent for Americans in the 45–54 age bracket. It's even higher as people get older.

But these basic statistics describe only what people are currently doing about their net worth, not what they *should* be doing if their goal is to maximize their lifetime enjoyment. So what *should* you be doing?

This is where my advice diverges from what most people do: You should find that one special point in your life when your net worth is *the highest it will ever be.* I call that point your net worth peak, or just "your peak."

Why should there ever be a peak—why can't your net worth just keep going up? First, remember that, from my perspective, your overarching goal is to maximize your lifetime fulfillment—to convert your life energy to as many experience points as you can. Doing that requires figuring out the optimal allocation of your money and free time to the right ages, given the inevitability of declining health and eventual death. As a result, some years you need to save very little money (so that you can spend more on your meaningful life experiences), while other years you should save more money (so that you will have more money to enjoy more, or better, experiences later).

But there's an even more important reason for a net worth peak: your goal is to die with zero. If your net worth keeps climbing, rising from your sixties to your seventies and beyond, then there is no way you will die with zero. So, at some point you must actually start dipping into your lifetime savings; if you don't, you will end up with unspent money, which means you haven't acquired as many experience points as you could have. That is why I say your net worth reaches a level at which it is the highest it should ever be—after which you must start spending it down on experiences while you can still extract a lot of enjoyment from those experiences. That point, in effect, is your peak.

You can't leave the timing of the peak to chance—to get the most out of your money and your life, you must *deliberately* determine the date of your peak. Later in this chapter I will give you some guidance on how to know and pinpoint that date.

But Will You Have Enough to Live On?

Before you start thinking about spending down your money, you must make sure you have enough to live on for the rest of your life. That's an important caveat, because plenty of people aren't saving enough for retirement. Although I want to urge everyone to maximize their experiences, I don't want to encourage irresponsible spending. Thinking of your peak as a date—and not as a number—is good advice only for people who have reached a certain savings threshold.

Even then, bear in mind that I am basing these recommendations on my own modeling of what makes for a fulfilling life; I am not a financial adviser, and if I inspire you to think differently about how to manage your money, it's a good idea for you to first work out the details of your personal situation with a professional, such as a certified financial planner or accountant.

With that disclaimer in place, let me explain how I approach and think about the savings threshold. The threshold I'm talking about—how much you need to save at a bare minimum—*is* a number. But as you'll see in a moment, that number may well be lower than what dutiful savers are already on track to save. That's because the threshold is based on avoiding the worst-case scenario (that is, running out of money before you die); it's the amount of money you need to have saved up *just to survive* without any other income. Once you meet this threshold, you don't need to work for money—and you can start carefully dipping into your savings.

So what is that threshold? Well, it's not the same number for everybody, because the cost of living varies based upon where you live, among other factors. And if you're supporting people other than yourself, you obviously will need more savings than if you are a family of one. But for everybody, the survival threshold is based on both your annual cost of living and the number of years you expect to live from the present day.

Let's look at an example. Let's assume your annual cost of survival is $12,000. That's admittedly really low. But I am using this example not to tell you specifically how much you will need but just to give you a feel for how the basic calculation works.

Let's also assume for this example that you are 55 years old and that, having looked at a life expectancy calculator, you expect to live until you're 80. So your money will have to last you another 25 years (that is, *years left to live* = 25). How much do you need in your nest egg *today* to have a survival amount for the rest of your life?

Well, to get a very rough answer—not the final answer—you would just multiply your annual cost of survival, the *cost to live one year,* by the number of years you'll be spending that amount, *years left to live*:

(cost to live one year) × (years left to live) = \$12,000 × 25 = \$300,000

Again, this is *not* the final answer. The real amount you need to save up is actually much lower than \$300,000. Why? Because your nest egg doesn't just sit there while you dip into it year after year. Assuming you've invested it in a typical stock/bond portfolio, your money is usually earning interest, working to bring in income even when you are no longer working. Therefore, whatever interest it's earning above inflation (whether that interest is 2 percent or 5 percent or whatever) is helping to offset the cost of your withdrawals.

Time for another disclaimer: Always bear in mind that even a stock/bond portfolio does not always earn interest above inflation. Rates of return can vary from year to year, sometimes by quite a bit.

For the sake of this example, though, let's assume an interest rate of 3 percent above inflation. And let's extend the example to take that 3-percent-above-inflation interest into account.

Suppose you start with $212,000 in savings and you spend $12,000 your first year. How much do you end up with after the first year? Well, you *don't* end up with just $200,000. Instead you end up with closer to $206,000, because even if you withdrew the entire $12,000 at the beginning of the year (such that the first $12,000 earns you no interest), the 3 percent you earn on the remaining $200,000 earns you a full $6,000. You can extend this process out for the same annual withdrawals and the same annual interest for the full 25 years.

This fixed annual withdrawal is an annuity (much like the annuities you can buy from an insurance company), and there's a technical formula (called the present value formula for an annuity) for calculating how much you'd need to start with to generate a given annuity. If you were to plug these numbers into that formula, you would find that the initial $212,000 will last you nearly until the end. (To be precise, you need to start with $213,210.12 if you want your money to last 25 years at 3 percent interest and a $12,000 annual withdrawal.) With each withdrawal, your initial amount does shrink—it just doesn't shrink as much as you might think, because the interest earns you back part of what you need. This is why you need only a portion of the annual cost of survival times the number of years: Interest will earn you the rest.

So what is that fraction? As a simple rule of thumb, I suggest 70 percent. In our example above, the fraction is actually just over 71 percent (because $213,210.12 is 0.7107 times $300,000). If the interest rate were higher, the fraction you'd need in savings would be lower. For example, if your interest rate is 5 percent, and everything else remains the same, you need only $173,426.50 —or a little less than 58 percent. And, of course, if the interest rate is zero, you'd need all of the money (the full $300,000) to come from savings alone. But 70 percent covers you in most cases, and it's a nice, simple number.

So let's capture all of this in one basic formula for calculating your survival threshold:

survival threshold = 0.7 × (cost to live one year) × (years left to live)

You can play around with different values of *cost to live one year* and *years left to live*. For example, if you want to retire in Florida, you can do some research to see what that would cost each year. And, of course, you can plug in a higher or lower number of years, too, and see the effect of these changes on your survival threshold.

Again, keep in mind that this survival threshold is the bare minimum. Once you've met that survival threshold, you probably won't want to retire just yet—it still might make sense for you to keep working to earn money for a higher quality of life than the basic survival threshold can provide. But now you can safely start thinking about at least the *possibility* of cracking open your nest egg. Once you've taken care of your worries about mere survival, you can then start thinking about your net worth peak as a date rather than a number.

Keep in mind, too, that you can use multiple sources of assets toward reaching your survival threshold. That is, if you have equity in your house, you can decide to downsize and sell the house—or, if you'd prefer to stay in your current home, you can take out a reverse mortgage, one way to tap into the value of your property. If you're unsure how many years the money must last you or are worried about running out, remember that you can take all or part of your savings to buy an annuity.

Knowing Your Peak: It's a
Date, Not a Number

Okay, let's say you have met your survival threshold and then some. Now you can afford to think of about when to break open your nest egg for maximum lifetime fulfillment. Again, when you think of your net worth peak this way, the peak is not a number (a specific dollar amount) but *a specific date* (tied to your biological age). Those are two very different ways of thinking about your financial goals.

Many of us have been trained to think that our plan for drawing down our savings should be framed in terms of numbers—that is, that once we reach a certain amount in savings, we can then retire and start living off those savings. And there's no shortage of suggestions about what that number should be. The most simplistic advice, which can't possibly be right, is for everyone to aim for a single number, such as $1 million or $1.5 million, no matter who you are or where you live. (How can $1 million in savings be the right number for both the healthy, world-traveling person living in San Francisco and the quiet homebody living in, say, Omaha?) No real retirement expert would suggest a one-size-fits-all number.

Instead, these experts give more personalized advice—basing the recommended number on your actual cost of living, your life expectancy, and projected interest rates (such as a typical annual 4.5 percent rate of return after inflation). Some advisers even take into account the fact that your retirement spending won't be constant from the start of retirement until its end—thus they tell you that you will need more money at the start of retirement (your go-go years) than when you're 10 or 20 years in. So there are definitely various degrees of sophistication in all this retirement-planning advice. But what all this financial advice has in common is the idea of coming up with a single number—one financial target to shoot for and hit before you can safely start to draw down your savings.

For those people who haven't saved enough to live on in retirement—either because their income is too low or because they've been too much of a grasshopper—the focus on reaching a financial target does make sense. Without such a pinpointed target in mind, people who haven't saved enough clearly risk ending up living out everyone's worst-case scenario: running out of money and then being too old to go back to work.

But a number should *not* be most people's main goal. One reason is that, psychologically, no number will ever feel like enough. For example, let's say the number you come up with (based on calculations like the kind financial advisers recommend) is $2 million. To reach that goal, you can easily justify working longer by telling and convincing yourself that you will be able to enjoy an even higher quality of life if you save up $2.5 million. And by that logic, you can provide for an even higher quality of life by saving $3 million. So where does it end? That's one problem with a numerical target. To try to keep up with this moving target, you just keep working on autopilot and end up postponing the best experiences of your life.

To understand why you should think in terms of a date, not a number, you need to recall that enjoying experiences requires a combination of money, free time, and health. You need all three—money alone is never enough. And for most people, accumulating more money takes time. So by working more years to build up more savings than you actually need, you are getting more of something (money), *but* you are losing even more of something *at least* as valuable (free time and health). Here's the bottom line: More money doesn't equal more experience points.

Most people forget those costs of acquiring more money, so they focus mainly on the gains. So, for example, $2.5 million does buy you a better quality of life than $2 million, *all other things being equal*—but all other things are usually *not* equal! That's because for every additional day you spend working, you sacrifice an equivalent amount of free time, and during that time your health gradually declines, too. If you wait five years to stop saving, your overall health declines by five years, closing the window on certain experiences altogether. In sum, from my per-

Declining Utility of Money with Age

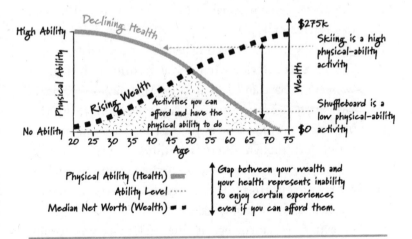

Your ability to enjoy experiences depends on both your economic ability (the wealth curve shown here) and your physical ability (the health curve). Continuing to build wealth doesn't necessarily buy you more experiences, because your declining health limits your enjoyment of certain experiences no matter how much money you have.

spective, the years you spend earning that extra $500,000 do not make up for (let alone surpass) the number of experience points you lost by working for more money instead of enjoying those five years of free time.

So, beyond a certain minimum financial survival amount, do *not* think in terms of a dollar amount. Think of your net worth peak as a date instead.

Of course, some people already think about when to stop growing their savings in terms of a date. The most obvious dates are age 62 (the earliest date you can choose to start collecting Social Security benefits) and age 65 (when you become eligible for Medicare). And, depending on when you were born, you can start receiving your full Social Security benefits somewhere between 66 and 67. Increasingly, given rising life expectancies, retirement experts recommend that middle-income retirees wait until they're 70 to claim Social Security benefits, at which point they can receive more than 100 percent of their full benefits. Now, the date you start collecting benefits and the date you retire don't have to coincide—but Social Security and Medicare dates *do* seem to have an effect on people's choice of retirement age, particularly because Social Security benefits make up a big chunk of most people's retirement income. The benefits don't tell the full story, though: Almost two-thirds of American workers say they plan to work past 65, according to 2016 research by the Pew Charitable Trusts. That is people's *projected* retirement age, not their actual retirement age.

The actual retirement age is often lower, because people sometimes retire before they planned to—usually because of unexpected job loss or illness. Such involuntary retirement is not an insignificant consideration, since it appears to affect more than half of all retirees in recent years: According to a study of nearly 14,000 newly retired workers, 39 percent who retired in 2014 were forced to quit, and another 16 percent were "partially forced." These numbers, if correct, show that many more Americans retire involuntarily than the official retirement statistics show. Age discrimination against older workers, combined with the stigma of involuntary job loss, apparently causes some workers to say they've retired when in fact they were merely forced out of their jobs and couldn't find another. Whatever the reason, the most common retirement age in the United States is actually 62, as is the median—again, the age at which Americans can start collecting Social Security benefits.

So when should you actually plan to crack open your nest egg? Put another way, if your net worth peak is a date, what is that all-important date? Well, it's tied to your biological age, which is just a measure of your overall health. If you take two 50-year-olds (that's their chronological age), one might have the biological age of a 40-year-old while the other has the biological age of a 65-year-old. The first, "younger" 50-year-old (let's call her Anne) not only will go on to live longer than the "older," less healthy 50-year-old (Betty) but will also be able to enjoy both physical and mental activities until an older age. With more good years ahead in which to enjoy experiences, Anne should be aiming for a later peak than Betty—which means that Anne will need to keep adding to her savings longer than Betty does before she can start spending down her net worth on the way to zero.

In researching this topic, my colleagues and I have now run the earning and spending simulations for dozens of hypothetical people like Anne and Betty, incorporating different scenarios about one's health, earning growth, and interest rates. Depending on all these factors, we see different net worth curves. As a result, we've generated lots of different net worth curves—each

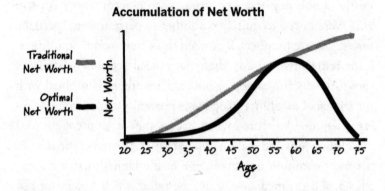

Traditionally, people continue to increase their net worth until they stop working, and are afraid to dip much into their principal even after retirement. But to make the most of your hard-earned money, you must crack open your nest egg earlier (starting to spend down your savings sometime between 45 and 60 for most people) so that you end, theoretically, with zero.

one optimal for a given person. In each optimal curve, the person ends up dying with exactly zero, and, because of that, each ends up with a net worth peak sometime before their death date. Here's what we see: For most people, the optimal net worth peak occurs at some point between the ages of 45 and 60.

Let's look at that more closely. First, let me make clear that 45 through 60 are chronological ages. As noted with the example of Anne and Betty, if a person's health is excellent (so their biological age is lower than their chronological age), the peak is on the higher end of that range. For the ultra-healthy, the real outliers, the peak might be even higher than 60. And, obviously, if someone has an illness that portends early death, then their peak occurs before age 45. But in general, most people hit their peak between the ages of 45 and 60. That's what our simulations show: For most people, waiting until they are past this age range causes suboptimal fulfillment results, because they end up dying with more than zero, running out of time in which to have many fulfilling experiences.

Clearly, earnings growth also has a big effect on a person's peak. Someone with rapid earnings growth hits their peak early. At the other end of the earnings spectrum are people who need to keep adding to their savings into their late sixties, perhaps even later, if they are to have any discretionary experiences after retirement. But again, in general, most people hit their peak between 45 and 60.

What does all this mean for you? It means that unless you are an exception, you ought to start spending your wealth down much earlier than what is traditionally recommended. If you wait until you're 65 or even 62 to dip into your nest egg, you will almost certainly end up working longer than necessary for money you will never get to spend. What a sad thought: to slave away at a job and never get the gold.

Don't get me wrong: I'm not telling you when you should retire—as I explain in the next section—only when you should start spending more than you earn.

"But I Love My Job!" Part II

When I first talked about dying with zero, I told you about the people who will understandably protest that they enjoy their work—so what's the harm with money earned from that kind of "work enjoyment" and seeing it going unused in your life? As I already said there, optimization doesn't care where the money comes from—once you get the money, you owe it to yourself to spend it wisely.

A version of this question comes up when I talk about spending down once you hit your peak: "What, do you really expect me to quit a job I love just because I've hit some magical date?" And my answer is no. If you want to keep working, be my guest. Just be sure to ramp up your spending accordingly so that you don't end up dying with lots of money left over. That would be a waste no matter how much you enjoyed your job.

I know there are a few lucky souls among us who are indeed "living the dream" and they are doing in life what they always dreamed of doing. These are those rare individuals who can't wait to get to work each day and who feel bad when they have to go home at night. They truly love what they are doing. But again, those individuals are few and far between. You may be one of them. But if you're not one of the lucky ones—if you're more in love with the paycheck you bring home than with the daily experiences of being in your office—then the time has come to do a real gut check on your life and to determine what you really want to get out of it.

Our culture's focus on work is like a seductive drug. It takes all of your yearning for discovery and wonder and experiences, promising to give you the means (money) to get all those things —but the focus on the work and the money becomes so single-minded and automatic that you forget what you were yearning for in the first place. The poison becomes the medicine—that's nuts!

Look, if all you want is to have a pile of money at the end, well, I guess that's your choice. But bear in mind that I have never seen somebody's total net worth posted on their tombstone. Wouldn't you rather try and figure out what unique experiences you'd like to have for your own, as personal keepsakes for down the road—not only for you but for your family and loved ones? This is precisely why I decided to splurge for that big 45th birthday party.

I have had this conversation with my friend Andy Schwartz. Andy's a successful entrepreneur in the adhesives business—glue. He's in his mid-fifties, married with three children in their twenties and teens, and has no plans to retire even though he could. He's got lots of reasons: The work continues to challenge and engage him intellectually, he loves spending time with others in his industry, and he feels responsible for the financial well-being of his employees. "If I didn't like it, if I felt like it was a chore, I would sell it and get out," he says.

So Andy is not somebody who's working simply because he's afraid he won't have enough to retire on. He loves the business, and he enjoys growing it—the business itself is a rich source of life experiences for him.

If you ask him why he likes growing his wealth, given that he is already wealthy, he'll mention his grandchildren, for whom he wants to provide a cushion, and charities to which he'd like to give money, such as his high school and college.

"Fine," I say. "I'm glad you're content. So continue working and earning more money—but be sure to spend it now! If you want to give money to your high school or college, do it now. If you want to give money to your children and future grand-children, start to do it now. (For children who are currently too young, set up a trust.) As for the rest, spend it on making the best life you possibly can for yourself."

When I tell Andy this, he says his tastes aren't expensive. He claims he leads a fairly quiet and modest lifestyle. To that I say, "How do you know what your tastes are if you really haven't done much except work and raise kids?" The truth is, Andy's business has been such a big part of his life and demanded so much of his attention that he is just not in the frame of mind to think about unique, novel, or stimulating ways to spend his money.

But if someone challenged him to spend, say, $300,000 on activities that are totally not work-related but actually fun-related, he'd be forced to think differently—and he would definitely discover new activities and pursuits he would love. And I'm not talking about spending money just for the sake of spending the money, either, but to become the fullest and most fulfilled version of Andy that he could be.

For starters, he and his wife could put their heads together and list their three favorite musical groups. Why not fly out to see them in some destination locale for a weekend? Or he could join TED as a patron member, which costs several hundred thousand dollars and gives you special access to the main TED conference, where he could meet living intellectual legends in many fields. After one trip to TED and talking to these amazing people, he could find 13 different purposes and directions he could go in!

Trust me—it's really not that hard to spend a lot of money doing things you love. But you do have to take some time to first consciously figure out what those appealing expenditures are for you. Using himself as an example of this idea, the behavioral economist Meir Statman has said that he finds travel by business class worth every penny—but doesn't feel that way about fine dining at all. "I can afford a $300 meal, but it makes me feel stupid—like the chef is in the back laughing uproariously." The point is that what you spend money on is up to you. Isn't it worth your while to think about what you value and put your money behind that?

So if you aren't ready to quit your job but want to make the most of your money before you die, start spending more than you have been!

Another strategy for squeezing the most experiences out of your early golden years without quitting your job is to cut back on your work hours if you can. If you're lucky enough to be working for an employer that offers a formal "phased retirement" program, definitely look into it. Unfortunately, only about 5 percent of all employers offer such programs, according to a 2017 report by the U.S. Government Accountability Office. However, the percentages are higher in some industries, such as education and high tech. The good news is that many more employers have informal programs, with managers offering phased retirement to high performers and employees with in-demand skills. It makes sense: The more valuable you are to your current employer, the more likely it is that they'll be willing to work with you on your terms.

In short, be careful not to be constantly seduced by money. Sure, it's nice to feel appreciated and to be paid well, and employers who value you might tempt you to work longer hours than would be optimal for you. It's easy to succumb to such temptation: After all, if you are 55 and a valued worker, chances are you're earning more per hour than you've ever earned before. But remember that your goal isn't to maximize wealth but rather to maximize *your life experiences.* That's a big turnabout for most people.

The Challenge of Decumulation

Once you've finally determined your net worth peak, you must start spending down, or decumulating. This means you will be spending more in your real golden years, when you are in rea-

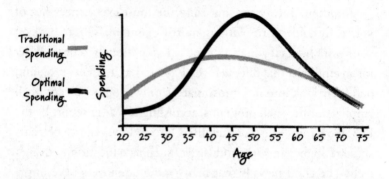

Spending Over Lifetime

Whether you are spending optimally or spending the way most people
spend, your spending in old age is lower than in the middle years, because
older people usually don't have the health needed to spend as much
on experiences. As a result, unless you spend significantly more in your
middle years than most people do, you will fail to die with zero.

sonably good shape in both health and wealth—between 45
and 60—than people usually do, because most people who save
money for the future save for too late in life.

Now think back to the concept of time buckets. When I first
introduced that tool, I urged you to set aside any concerns about
money so that you could see that most experiences naturally fall
on a bell-shaped curve that leans a little to the left, your younger
years. But what happens when you do begin to put price tags on
the experiences you want to have? At that point, the curve will
right itself a little, because as your health starts its natural decline, your wealth tends to increase, which means you have more
discretionary income for higher-quality experiences. For example, if you enjoy both movies and live theater, you can do either
at just about any age, which means you can happily spread them

out throughout your life. But once you start thinking about money, you can no longer ignore the fact that theater tickets usually cost a whole lot more than movie tickets, which means that, to get the most enjoyment, you'll want to shift some of the experiences of live theater to the right, when you're older and wealthier. But you *don't* want to shift them too far to the right, to the point where you'll be too old to hear the actors or to stand in line for the restroom; at that point in your life, you'd just as soon stay home watching *Jeopardy* or reruns of *The Golden Girls*.

There's another conclusion you'll probably reach when you start putting price tags on these experiences: The amount of money you'll need in retirement is often a lot lower than what you've been advised to save. For example, if you've been told that during each year of retirement you will need 80 percent or more of your annual pre-retirement income, you will probably discover, after looking at the activities you've bucketed for your seventies, eighties, and beyond, that these really don't cost that much—far less than 80 percent of your previous spending. (Recall the research on the no-go years from chapter 3.) It's true that some physically undemanding activities—like attending the opera—can be pricey, but you probably don't even want to go to the opera 70 times within a period of just five years. At a certain point in life, you simply won't be able to consume above a certain amount of savings—so don't save too much, and instead plan to enjoy spending that money sooner.

But even when you include money as a consideration, the curve won't skew right—you will find that the vast majority of the experiences you want to have will have to happen within about 20 years of midlife, in either direction—in other words, roughly between 20 and 60. People so often talk about saving for retirement. But there are far fewer conversations about saving for excellent and memorable life experiences that need to happen much sooner than the typical retirement age. If you look at the activities that are advertised in retirement commercials—a couple holding hands while strolling on a beautiful beach, a man holding a youngster on his shoulders—you'll find that you actually want to do most of those things before you're retired.

Am I telling you to blow all your money before 60? No. You'll definitely need income when you're older, too—so while you're still working to earn money, you'd better save for that time in your life when you'll no longer be working. Just realize that time moves in only one direction, and that as it passes it sweeps away opportunities for certain experiences forever. If you keep that in mind as you plan your future, you'll be more likely to make the best use of every year of time in your life.

Knowing that you have enough money to last you the rest of your life (by doing some survival calculations) should give you the peace of mind to start spending more aggressively now. But even so, the psychological shift from savings mode to spending mode won't be easy. Changing one's deeply entrenched habits never is: If you've spent all your life as a good, solid, and committed saver, it's hard to suddenly shift gears and start doing just the opposite. For people used to accumulating wealth, decumulation doesn't come naturally. Old habits die hard.

But doing this is absolutely essential if you are going to make the most of your life energy. Remind yourself that you can't take your money with you—every dollar you don't spend at the right time will have far less value to you later, and in some cases it will bring you no enjoyment at all.

Remember, too, to invest in your health, even if you haven't done much of that in the past. As I explained earlier, your health massively changes your ability to enjoy all kinds of experiences.

So it's well worth your while to spend time and money improving or at least maintaining your health, whether by joining a ritzy gym (the kind you actually look forward to visiting), hiring a personal trainer, or following along with fitness videos.

One of my sisters, Tia, has really taken this advice to heart. At 57, she still works in her family's business, but she redesigned the way she does her job so she no longer sits in a chair for nine or ten hours a day like she used to. She understands that everyone's muscles atrophy with age, and she's slowing down the rate of that decline by doing resistance training several times a week. She also regularly swims and takes a spin class. She's on it! Tia's not going to run a marathon anytime soon—but through these investments in her health, she's actively changing her current and future experience of life.

Re-Bucket Your Life

As you go through life, your interests change and new people enter your life, so it's a good idea to repeat the time-bucketing exercise every now and then, such as every five or ten years.

One of the most important times to re-bucket your life is when you're nearing your net worth peak. Many people at midlife have forgotten what used to bring them fulfillment and have been too busy taking care of careers and children to explore new interests, either. As a result, many people enter retirement with only a vague idea of what they'll do with all that free time. Or they have some specific ideas—typically trips they want to take—but only for the first year or two. So after a while, they tend to find themselves adrift, feeling aimless and maybe even itching to go back to work, the one place they know they'll have a built-in sense of purpose, belonging, and accomplishment. In the worst cases, this sense of aimlessness can even lead to anxiety and depression.

So before you quit or scale back your job, really think through what you want to do once your work won't be taking up much of your everyday time. Is there a long-dormant hobby you want to pick up again? A particular friendship you want to rekindle? A new skill you want to learn, or a club you want to join? What adventures do you really want to have—and when do you want to have them? Put those in the appropriate buckets and start making new memories.

Recommendations

- Calculate your *annual survival cost* based on where you plan to live in retirement.
- Consult your doctor to get a read on your biological age and mortality; get all the objective tests you can afford that give you the status of your current health and eventual decline.
- Given your own health and history, think about when your enjoyment of those activities is likely to start declining in a noticeable way on an annual basis—and how the activities you love will be affected by this decline.

9

BE BOLD — NOT FOOLISH

Rule No. 9:
Take your biggest risks when
you have little to lose.

Mark Cuban, the owner of the Dallas Mavericks and one of the investor "sharks" on *Shark Tank,* learned entrepreneurship at a young age. At 12, he was selling trash bags to his neighbors. At 16, he was buying stamps and then reselling them for profit. Growing up in a working-class family in Pittsburgh, he remembers his mom urging him to learn a trade, like laying carpet. Instead, Cuban went to study business management in college, which he paid for by giving disco dance lessons and eventually buying and running a campus pub. As it turned out, police went on to shut down the pub for underage drinking, and when Cuban graduated, he was still broke—but he now had the skills and confidence to make it in business. So after a short stint working for a bank in his hometown, the 23-year-old Cuban packed his meager belongings into an old Fiat and drove to Dallas, joining a friend from college who'd sung the city's praises. There, the two shared an apartment with four other guys, where Cuban's bed was a sleeping bag on a beer-stained carpet in the living room. But he kept hustling. He got a job as a bartender, and another as a salesman in a software store.

And when he got fired for defying the boss at the store, he hatched plans for his own company—a computer consulting business called MicroSolutions. A few years later, when he was 32, he sold that company for $6 million and retired for five years.

Bet When You Have Nothing (or Little) to Lose

Eventually, Cuban came out of his early retirement and started the business that made him a multi-billionaire—but that's really beside the point here. What's most interesting to me about Mark Cuban's experience is that none of the bold moves that led to this success felt risky to him—not the move to Dallas or the jobs he took there, not defying his boss, and not the business he started after getting fired. "I had nothing," he recalled. "So I had nothing to lose, right? It was all about going for it."

What Cuban is saying is that he was facing a situation of asymmetric risk: when the upside of possible success is much greater than the downside of possible failure. When you face asymmetric risk, it makes total sense to be bold, to grab the opportunity at hand. At the extreme, when the downside is very low (or nonexistent, as in the "nothing to lose" case) and the upside is really high, it's actually riskier *not* to make the bold move. The downside of not even taking a chance is emotional: potentially a lifetime of regret and wondering *What if?* The upside of taking a chance always includes emotional benefits—even if things don't work out. There's a great sense of pride at having pursued an important goal wholeheartedly. If you've given something your all, you'll get a lot of positive memories out of the experience no matter what happens. That's just another form of the memory dividend I talked about earlier: When you look back from any point during your life, you will remember your actions in a positive light. In other words, even experiences that don't end the way you'd hoped can still yield positive memory dividends. So being bold is an investment in your future happiness—and therefore another way to maximize the area under the curve.

Most opportunities don't present an extreme asymmetry of risk, but if you think them through, you'll often see that the downside isn't as high as you might think.

The Younger You Are, the Bolder You Should Be

Bear in mind what I said about investing in experiences, especially when you're young. The idea is that it's always good to invest in experiences—but it's especially good to do it when you're young. Well, a similar logic applies to being bold: When you're older, some risks become more foolish than bold.

This is easy to see with physical risks. When I was a kid, I used to jump off the roof of my garage. It was fun, and I never got really hurt. It didn't even feel like a risk. But I'd be a fool to try jumping off a roof now, with my 50-year-old body: I'm heavier, and my knees aren't as good at absorbing shocks. So if I did jump, I'd probably end up in the doctor's office—and even if the injury didn't cause lasting damage, I would take a long time to recover from it. In other words, I have much more to lose than to gain from a jump like that. So my days of leaping off the top of my garage are behind me.

That happens in a lot of areas, where the balance between risk and reward changes with time—until the window of opportunity is gone forever. When you're young, every risk you take can pay off in a big way if you succeed: Your upside is huge. At the same time, the downside (in other words, what happens when you take the risk and fail) is low, because you have a lot of time to recover. In poker, for example, you can sometimes buy more chips, or "reload." Well, when you're young, you're at a stage in the game of life when you can reload and reload and reload.

As a result, the long-term impact of any failure ends up being pretty low. When I was 23, I got fired from my job as a junior trader at an investment bank. In that job, I had been in training for the career I wanted, but one day I came in to work tired and was caught resting my head in the booth. Well, that was the end of that job. I was scared and uncertain about what I'd do next, and it was no fun being unemployed for the next month. My unemployment ended when I took a job as a broker—a job that paid well but was not what I really wanted to do, which was trading. Still, I knew I had to do something, and I figured I would see where this broker journey led. I was 23—it was easy to correct course. Even if I hadn't found the broker job, even if

I were an abject failure, I wasn't going to die, and I wasn't heading for a soup line.

Notice that I'm not saying that being bold in situations of asymmetric risk always leads to success, the way it did for Mark Cuban. Sometimes things don't go your way, no matter how hard you try. What I'm saying is that the "loss" is worth it— it was still a good bet because I knew I had little to lose, I had plenty of time to course-correct, and I still acquired some great memories.

Career Choices

Let's say you want to become an actor, but you know it's an intensely competitive field: Most people who move to Hollywood never make it and end up waiting tables between auditions. Your alternative to pursuing a career in acting is a safe office job that doesn't excite you. So should you leave your safe job behind to move to Hollywood? Well, it depends almost entirely on your age—not on what your parents are expecting of you or what your friends think you should do. If you're in your early twenties, you should go for it! Give it your all, really exhaust yourself trying for what you want. You can give yourself a few years, and if it doesn't work out, you can still go back to an office job—or to school to learn a trade.

That's exactly what former actor Jeff Cohen did when his acting career didn't pan out. If you've ever seen *The Goonies*, the 1985 movie about a group of kids on a quest for lost treasure, you probably remember the character named Chunk, the chubby member of the gang of misfits. Chunk was Cohen's breakthrough role—until that point, his career had consisted of small parts in TV shows and commercials. After *The Goonies*, the exuberant, funny Cohen seemed on track for a big career in Hollywood—but new roles failed to materialize. What happened? Puberty had turned him "from Chunk to hunk," Cohen likes to say with a laugh. Hollywood is full of sad stories of former child actors, but fortunately Cohen's story isn't one of them. He went on to college and law school, specialized in entertainment law, and is now a partner in his own firm. So what that his acting career fizzled?

If you're in your fifties, on the other hand, moving to Hollywood is not a great plan. At that point, chances are you now have people in your life who are truly depending on you, like a spouse and children. If that's the case, your failure is no longer your own—it affects other people. It's for the same reason that I stopped riding motorcycles and taking flying lessons once I had kids: In my mind, I no longer had the right to put my life on the line for the sake of those thrills. And so it is with all kinds of risks: The older you get, the more you have to lose. But it's not just that the stakes are higher. The potential rewards are also lower! So even if you're a lone wolf, or your kids are grown and flown, the risk/reward balance still isn't in your favor when you're older. In the best-case scenario, where things go spectacularly well for you, you'll have fewer years to enjoy that success. Wouldn't you rather have taken the big risk earlier in life?

I can't say it's foolish for anybody to start pursuing their dreams in their fifties, because everybody's circumstances are different; and if you missed your chance to do what you wanted when you were younger and you see your upcoming retirement years as your last chance to follow your dreams, I'd say it's better late than never. But if we could go back in time, I would say:

Don't wait. Do the bold thing now, rather than in retirement, because the go-go years are very short. In general, this whole "I'll wait to do this when I'm retired" is a massive blunder. But if you've already made that blunder, go ahead and make the most of the time you've got.

But so many people don't take advantage of those times when they *can* easily take risks. And I think it's because they magnify the downside in their minds—they think of the absolutely worst-case scenario, like homelessness, even if that scenario is not remotely realistic. As a result of that kind of fearful thinking, they don't recognize the asymmetry in the risk they are facing: In their minds, it's as if disastrous failure is as likely as any kind of success.

A couple of years ago I was talking to a young person I know named Christine who had a job selling plastic countertops. There's nothing inherently wrong with selling countertops, plastic or otherwise, and I'm sure some salespeople get great satisfaction from helping customers find exactly the right countertop for them. It's just that Christine wasn't one of them, mainly because her employer wasn't giving her recognition for all her hard work. She also had very few days off. The job was making her so unhappy that I urged her to take a bold move and just quit. Just quit, without even waiting to line up another job, because holding down that sales job left her with very little time to look for anything better. She was very afraid, though, that not having a job would make it hard for her to get a new job. It's true that employers are often wary of hiring people who are unemployed—so quitting her job was a risk. But I persuaded her that at 25, she was young enough to take the risk. She could get a job tomorrow waiting tables if she needed to, until she figured out what she really wanted to do. Her downside, in other words, was not as bad as she imagined. Besides, if she couldn't take the risk now, when could she take the risk?

She took my advice and quit without having another job lined up. She's since held a series of positions, including another job she hated but that paid $150,000 a year. (That job made her so miserable that she quit—but then came back to it two weeks later.) The point is that when you're young you can afford to take a lot of risks because you have plenty of time to recover—you can stumble and stumble your ass off and come back just fine.

Of course, it's always easier to quit when you have another job already lined up—but, as I said to Christine, what's easy shouldn't determine what you do. Don't let difficulty dissuade you from living your best life!

Quantify the Fear: The Case for Moving

One of the biggest ways people avoid bold action is an aversion to moving and travel. Many people won't even consider moving to a different city, and when an opportunity far from home does arise, I often hear them saying things like "I won't know anybody there" or "I want to stay close to my mom." It's amazing to me that people will root themselves and not seek any new life adventure because they are fearful of moving away from two or three people; if you do that, it's like letting those two or three people choose where you live.

It's not that you shouldn't care about maintaining relationships. It's that if you think about the problem rationally, you might discover that you can have the adventure and still maintain wonderful relationships, in addition to making new friends where you go. How do you think through this question rationally? My answer is to quantify every single fear.

For example, let's say you have an opportunity to move across the country (or across the world) for an exciting job that pays $70,000 a year more than your current job. But you're afraid you'll lose touch with your friends and family.

When I hear something like that, I ask a couple of questions. One is: How much time do you spend with these people? Often it's not that much time at all, because we tend to take for granted what is readily available. The other question I ask is: How much is a round-trip first-class ticket from here to there on no notice? This is the highest price you would have to pay to see the people you'd be moving away from. So how does that price compare with your salary gain, not to mention everything else you stand to gain from moving? Even after doing these calculations, people still sometimes decide to stay put. That's their choice, of course, but I want to point out that what they are doing is saying that they are willing to pay $70,000 for the comfort of not having to move.

If I had never been willing to move, I would have passed up the biggest career opportunity of my life. This happened when I was 25 and working as an over-the-counter broker, the job I was hired for after getting fired two years earlier. As a natural gas broker, I was making good money, about 10 to 15 times what I was earning in my first job out of college. And I was having fun with my higher salary—but I hated that job. I hated having to cold-call people, and I found it distasteful that my success was so dependent on whether a particular person I was calling liked me or not. Also, the nature of being a broker was that my upside was capped no matter how well I performed. I had some control, but not as much as I wanted. That's why I wanted to be a trader. If a broker is like a real estate agent, a trader is like the person who buys and sells houses: As a trader, you take all the risk and get all the reward.

The opportunity to become a trader came unexpectedly. As part of my broker job, I was making what I thought was a routine trip to visit a customer in Texas. Little did I know that I was actually being interviewed: At the end of my visit, my customer offered me the job of head options trader at his company! I remember negotiating with him, as if I were not sure this was a job I wanted to take, but in the back of my head I was thinking, *Where are my bags? I'm ready to move!*

Other people didn't understand why I'd want to leave a cushy job in New York City to take a job so risky that I didn't know if I'd make any money—and to move to Texas, of all places! I'll admit I had my own stereotypes about Texas, or anywhere south of the Mason-Dixon Line, really—especially as a black person. But my desire for the potential riches that being a trader could bring was so great that I would do anything for the chance to try. I would move to Siberia if I had to. I also knew that I'd hate myself if I didn't take the job. And what did I really have to lose? If it didn't work out, I could have gone back to New York City and become a broker again. And knowing that I had tried it would make me proud of myself for the rest of my life, and would make me feel that my life was more meaningful. In this way, even "negative" experiences can bring positive memory dividends. High upside, low downside.

Everything happened to work out: I succeeded as a trader and came to love Texas. A week after arriving for my job in

Houston, my manager and I went to a charity auction at which we bid on a horse and on a shotgun. So for a while I co-owned a horse, which my friends back in New York thought was bizarre. I no longer own a horse, but I still have that classic shotgun. And while I still maintain friendships with people I met and knew in New York, I've built a happy life and found plenty of like-minded people in Houston too.

I know that, reading all this, you might be feeling tempted to dismiss my experience: *Easy for you to say, Bill.* Not everybody gets offers to make a ton of money in trading, and certainly not everyone has a cushy job to leave in the first place. But the logic of my experience works at any scale, from someone who leaves a six-figure job and can borrow money from their rich parents to guys who have only two nickels to rub together. The guy working at Burger King who takes night classes to learn computer programming, or the woman who joins forces with a friend to start a food truck business—that's being bold, too, just on a smaller scale. In all these cases, you can take the safer path of quiet misery or the bolder path that's less certain but potentially much more rewarding, both financially and psychologically.

How to Be Bold as an Older Person

Everything I've said in this chapter points to being bold when you're young. But there are ways to be bold as an older person, too. And those have to do with being brave enough to spend your hard-earned money. You have to have the courage to do the things I described in the "Know Your Peak" chapter—the courage to walk away from a career so that you can spend your remaining time doing what's more fulfilling. People are more afraid of running out of money than wasting their life, and that's got to switch. Your biggest fear ought to be wasting your life and time, not *Am I going to have* x *number of dollars when I'm 80?*

What If I'm Risk Averse?

I can understand the fear of risk because my mom is like that: She was a teacher, working for the state, and always wanted me to get a government job of some sort, too. We had so many arguments about that—so-called job security—her saying that a government job gave you a guarantee, a big measure of safety. I always wanted the opposite—to try to lasso the moon. I figured that if the post office was always hiring, and provided a safe income, I could always go work there if all else failed; but there's no need to *start* there.

Yet I understand where my mom was coming from: She's an African American woman who was born right after the Great Depression and lived for many years before the civil rights era. Life was always unfair and the world seemed out to get you, so it made sense that she was coming from a place of wanting safety before anything else. In fact, her mother—my grandmother—was even more fearful. I'll never forget what my mom said to me when I made my first million dollars. "Don't tell your grandmother," she told me, "because all she's going to do is worry about you losing it."

So I get how your upbringing can make you want to play it safe. People naturally vary in their risk tolerance, and that's okay.

I'm not going to tell you how much risk you should take on. But I will add this: First, whatever level of risk you're comfortable with, whatever bold moves you might contemplate for your life, you're generally better off making those moves earlier in your life. Again, that's when you have a higher upside and a lower downside.

Second, don't underestimate the risk of inaction. Staying the course instead of making bold moves feels safe, but consider what you stand to lose: the life you *could* have lived if you had mustered the courage to be bolder. You're gaining a certain kind of security, but you are also losing experience points. For example, realize that if you avoid certain risks, you will get 7,000 experience points instead of 10,000. That means you end up with a life that's 30 percent less fulfilling. If you say that 30 percent less fulfillment is worth the peace of mind you get, well, that's okay. My grandma, for example, wouldn't have been able to sleep at night if she'd lived a bolder life, and I can't fault her for that. How much risk you take on is your own personal choice — I just want you to be aware of the decision you're making and the full consequences of that choice.

Third, I'll remind you that there's a difference between low risk tolerance and plain old fear. Fear tends to take the actual risk and then blow it out of proportion. If you're prone to knee-jerk fear reactions to taking bold moves, think through the worst-case scenario. When you consider all the safety nets you've got in your life — from unemployment insurance provided by your job to private insurance you can buy against any kind of disaster to good old-fashioned help from your family — the worst-case scenario is probably not as bad as you think. If that's the case, your downside is usually quite limited — but your upside might be infinite.

Recommendations

- Identify opportunities that you're not taking that pose little to risk to you. Always remember that you're better off taking more chances when you are younger than when you're older.
- Look at the fears that are holding you back, rational or irrational. Don't let irrational fears get in the way of your dreams.
- Realize that at every moment you have a choice. The choices you make reflect your priorities, so be sure you're making those choices deliberately.

Conclusion:
An Impossible Task, a Worthy Goal

I've given you an impossible task: to die with zero. You can follow every rule in this book, you can closely track your health and life expectancy, and you can recalculate your financials every day —yet you're not going to hit exactly zero. When you take your last breath, you might still have a few dollars in your pocket, and maybe even hundreds more in the bank. So technically, you will have failed to die with zero. That's inevitable—and it's okay.

Why? Because that goal will have done its real job, of pushing you in the right direction: By aiming to die with zero, you will forever change your autopilot focus from earning and saving and maximizing your wealth to living the best life you possibly can. That's why dying with zero is a worthy goal—with this goal in mind, you are sure to get more out of your life than you otherwise would have.

Millions of people go to church or temple every week trying to be like Jesus or Moses; millions more try to emulate Muhammad. Most don't even come close. And that's okay—none of us is perfect, and even the most virtuous among us aren't always kind, always wise, always courageous. But by pursuing these ideals, we do move in the right direction—we become at least a little bit kinder, wiser, and more courageous. And so it is with the ideal of dying with zero: Try as you might, you will never hit the target exactly, but with any luck you will get closer than if you'd never tried. So go ahead—not only living your life to the fullest, but saving the only life you've got.

I hope my message has at least jarred you into rethinking the standard and conventional approaches to living one's life—get a good job, work hard through endless hours, and then retire in your sixties or seventies and live out your days in your so-called golden years.

But I still ask you: Why wait until your health and life energy have begun to wane? Rather than just focusing on saving up for a big pot full of money that you will most likely not be able to spend in your lifetime, live your life to the fullest *now:* Chase memorable life experiences, give money to your kids when they can best use it, donate money to charity while you're still alive. That's the way to live life.

Remember: In the end, the business of life is the acquisition of memories.

So what are you waiting for?

Acknowledgments

Everyone gets ideas: Often we have something we discuss ad nauseam, telling anyone who will listen, "I'm going to do x." Over the years, though, the x becomes another item we stash in our procrastination bucket, something that never gets done without an inciting incident. For me, that inciting incident was a visit to my doctor, Chris Renna, whose urgent enthusiasm for my message finally propelled me into action.

Before I could dream of writing a book and allowing the world to critique and consider my ideas, I first had to discuss, debate, and refine these ideas with the toughest audience I could find: My most straight-shooting friends, family, and colleagues. Each lent a unique and interesting perspective and told me when they thought I was crazy. I want to acknowledge (in no particular order) Tia Sinclair, Greg Whalley, John Arnold, Cooper Richey,

Marc Horowitz, Omar Haneef, and Dan Bilzerian for taking the time to hear me blather and to put my ideas to the test.

Having well-thought-out ideas is one thing, but converting those ideas into a convincing, easy-to-read book is another. For that I would need to work with a writer who could take my words, stories, and explanations and shape them into a flowing, easy-to-read text while retaining my voice, style, and passion. That writer was Marina Krakovsky. I was really lucky to have a writer who was familiar with the relevant ideas from economics and who had the ability to support these ideas with relevant academic research. She also knew my agent as well as Kay-Yut Chen, a brilliant economist whom I went on to hire for work on this book. I want to thank Marina not only for all this, but also for pushing me through the long, unfamiliar, and sometimes painful process of turning a complex series of ideas into a book anyone can understand.

Once I had a professional writer and a set of good ideas and what seemed like a strong proposal, I needed a publisher to help the book reach the widest possible audience. To find such a publisher, I needed an agent in my corner. That person is Jim Levine. Although five agents said they would take me on as a client based on the initial pitch, I chose Jim because he was the only one who told me that the proposal, while good, wasn't ready to show to publishers—and he explained clearly why he thought so. I want to thank Jim for his special interest in my work and his help in guiding me from being a guy with a book idea to a guy with an idea that's ready for a book deal.

I want to thank Rick Wolff and all of the Houghton Mifflin Harcourt team for investing in me and in this book. I also want to thank Rick for editing a book that doesn't fit easily into one genre, and for helping us get the ideas across without coming across as too pushy or strident. (I'm pushy and strident.)

Thanks also to Will Palmer, a copy editor who went above and beyond the usual work of a copy editor.

I also want to thank people in my office who took the time to take a survey to give much-needed perspective and to help me get past my myopia about how people view this subject. In no particular order, my thanks for doing this go to Charles Denniston, Oleg Kostenko, Barrie Nichols, Shilpa Chunchu, Loftus Fitzwater, and Cassandra Krcmar.

To help convey ideas in a relatable way, there's nothing like a story. In a book about how people should spend their money and their life, these stories are often highly personal, and I appreciate my friends, family, and acquaintances who let themselves be vulnerable by opening their lives to public scrutiny and criticism. So a big thanks to Erin Broadston Irvine, John Arnold, Baird Craft, Andy Schwartz, Jason Ruffo, Joe Farrell, Paulie "Pastrami" Simoniello, Christine Platania, Greg Whalley, Chris Riley, my sister Tia Sinclair, and my mom, Fruita Louise Diaz. A special thanks to Virginia Colin, who shared her story even though she did not know me. This book could not inspire or motivate anyone without your generous and courageous contributions.

Aside from relatable stories, I also needed a formal model—a mathematical representation—of the ideas I'm talking about. Behavioral economist Kay-Yut Chen was enormously helpful not only in working out the math behind the model but also in explaining the logic behind the results. Omar Haneef also played a key role in helping model these ideas.

The other data used in this book is publicly available, thanks to research by the U.S. government, but presenting it in an easy-to-read format is an entirely different task. Charles Denniston created every single chart and picture in this book. Whenever we swapped out data sources or requested other changes, Charles always quickly turned around just what we needed.

For maintaining my schedule, coordinating meetings, making sure I made my phone calls, and generally managing chaos, I want to thank my assistant, Cassandra Krcmar. I appreciate her keeping the circus of my life manageable during this process with her usual grace.

Many people read parts of this book and gave me feedback —but asking someone to read an unedited book and provide feedback, especially negative comments, is a particularly grueling favor. It takes many hours of attentive work and entails the dreaded responsibility of telling someone you know when something isn't good, or that it's wrong, arrogant, or just plain sucks. If you like this book, it's because of these hardworking, intrepid early readers. If you don't like the book, you would have hated it more if it weren't for Raquel Segal, Omar Haneef, Kay-Yut Chen, Keith Perkins, Marc Horowitz, and, most of all, Cooper Richey.

Cooper Richey actually deserves his own paragraph. If you think reading my unfinished book is a big favor, try reading it two and a half times! Try doing it while providing detailed page-by-page notes and criticisms. Try reading it and getting inspired to present more ideas, and then calling to discuss and debate some more. Try then getting recruited for additional suggestions. They say that no good deed goes unpunished, and I really punished Cooper. Seriously, he went above and beyond my original requests and provided more than significant contributions to make the book better than it was before. I'm extremely grateful for the extra time and effort he put into making this book better.

I want to thank my godfather, Joseph Panepinto, Esq., for opening one door of opportunity that led to this crazy, wonderful adventure.

Everything we build is on the shoulders of prior generations, and I'd like to thank my mom and dad, Fruita Louise Diaz and Bill Perkins Jr.

Writing the book has been a blur, so if I missed anyone, I apologize, and I thank you.

I can't count the number of hours spent just talking about the book or meeting about the book or thinking about the book, but clearly the result is that someone else was not getting my brain cycles during that time. My work is their sacrifice, and I couldn't have done this work without the love and patience of my kids, Skye and Brisa, as well as that of my girlfriend, Lara Sebastian, as they tolerated and endured my mental absence far too many times. Thank you! I'm back!

Appendix:
What Is This New App
You Keep Talking About?

The principles in this book are designed and presented to take you a long way toward getting more out of your money and your life. They give you some general guidelines on how to strike a healthy balance between present enjoyment and delayed gratification, between working for money (and investing it for future gains) and spending that money on the experiences that make for a rich, fulfilling life.

But maybe you want to go beyond following just the basic guidelines. To that end, I have some good news. The app that my team and I have developed aims to go a step further by taking those same principles and putting them in precise mathematical form. Earnings, expenditures, interest rates, experience points—all of these involve numbers and calculations. Optimizing across many possible combinations of such numbers—

as we must do to give you a plan for a maximally fulfilling life —requires far more calculations than anyone can perform in a reasonable amount of time. An app can do the necessary calculations faster and more accurately than even the most gifted accountant. And that's exactly what our app does: It takes in all these numbers and does all the calculations necessary to help you plan for the most experience-rich life you can have.

The description you read here covers the most essential features—but in each future version we will add more complexity, to match real-world scenarios.

What the App Does (and Doesn't Do)

As I explained earlier, my way of thinking about getting the most out of your life energy is to maximize the area under the fulfillment curve. But how do you maximize the area under that curve? It's not at all obvious, because we face an ongoing trade-off between spending and earning. For example, suppose we spend a full year playing rather than working for money. Well, we can earn a lot of life experience points that way—but we incur a big cost, too. Specifically, we sacrifice all of that year's financial earnings—as well as any bank interest or other investment returns that cash would have earned. All of that amounts to money that could be used for possibly even more experience points the following year. So the question is: Is it better to earn now and spend later? Or, more precisely: What is the right balance between earning and spending at any particular point in your life? That's not an easy question to answer.

As a result, most of us don't think about these trade-offs in a conscious way: We tend to either wing it or just follow simple rules of thumb, like "save 10 percent of your income every year" and "retire at 65." Or we wake up one day feeling burned out by too much work and too little play, and decide it's about time we take a real vacation. Some of us plan more than others, but I don't know anybody who plans out their entire life. For the most part, we go about these important decisions in a kind of willy-nilly way: earn a little money here, spend some there, save and invest some for next year or for retirement, and adjust our spending decisions as we go along from one year to the next. That's understandable, given how overwhelming the problem can seem, and following simple rules of thumb is better than not planning at all. But in truth, such an approach is not maximizing our life experiences.

My goal with the app is to maximize my lifetime fulfillment and yours—which means getting you as close as humanly possible to the best set of financial decisions you can make throughout your life.

But I don't want to exaggerate the app's capabilities. The results from a piece of software are only as good as the data we give it. Yet the world is complex and full of uncertainty. So crucial inputs for the app, including your future health and the rate of return on your investments, are hard to predict. In truth, the app is just another tool, much like the other tools in this book. It's a more precise and mathematical tool than, say, time buckets—yet it would be a serious mistake to confuse the app's precision with total accuracy.

A better way of thinking about the app is as a simulation engine: a way to run what-if scenarios about your life. For example, what if your income grows while your investment returns remain flat? And what happens if your health declines at a faster rate than most? By playing around with the app, you can explore what happens when you change this assumption or that one, and what effect tweaking this variable or that one has on your lifetime fulfillment score.

In other words, for each set of assumptions you want to consider, what is the optimal way for you to allocate your life energy to earning money versus acquiring experiences at different points in your life? The app can give you answers to this question under a variety of different possible scenarios.

Where to Get the App

As a reader of this book, you can get the app for free from the book's Web site: DieWithZeroBook.com.

How to Use the App

Using the app is relatively simple, because it will guide you every step of the way. It does this by asking you straightforward questions about those factors that go into determining your lifetime fulfillment score: questions about your current health, your free time, and your spending on life experiences. It also asks you about your income growth each year and the rate of return on your financial investments. These are the major variables that will help determine how much fulfillment you can glean from life. Along those lines, you will see why an app is so vitally important. It would be too exhausting, tedious, and time-consuming to do the calculations yourself, because you need to iterate through the fulfillment algorithm multiple times, once for every year of your life—updating your health score each year and taking some of the output from one year and using it as input for the next year, then trying to accurately add up the fulfillment scores from all those years. The magic of the app is that it can do all these calculations for you, quickly and easily.

Realize, too, that there isn't just one calculation to run. That's because your overall fulfillment score depends on your inputs, and these can vary. With this app, you can try out different inputs to see the effect on your total.

Finally, you can even let the simulation engine run wild. The whole point of the app is to help you spend your life energy in the most efficient, experience-maximizing way, which also means minimizing the amount of time you spend working for money you'll probably never get to enjoy. To figure out this optimal solution, you could play around with the app all day and still not find the best answer. So instead of trying out different scenarios yourself, you can put in some assumptions about the values of the variables you *cannot* control—and let the app run every possible simulation for you, then find the one with the highest fulfillment score and spit out the optimal values for the factors *within* your control that yielded that optimal result.

Everyone's answers will be different, and you might be in for some surprises, but one fundamental principle remains the same: Under no optimal combination of decisions do you ever end up with any money left over. If you want to maximize fulfillment in your life, ideally you need to use up all your money by the end. That is, of course, the basic idea behind Die with Zero.

Notes

1. OPTIMIZE YOUR LIFE

page

5 *As the title:* Amy Finkelstein, Erzo F. P. Luttmer, and Matthew J. Notowi-
   digdo, "What Good Is Wealth Without Health? The Effect of Health on the
   Marginal Utility of Consumption," *Journal of the European Economic Asso-
   ciation* 11 (2013): 221–58.

6 *vast resources before they die:* David Callahan, "The Richest Americans Are
   Sitting on $4 Trillion. How Can They Be Spurred to Give More of it Away?,"
   Inside Philanthropy, https://www.insidephilanthropy.com/home/2018/12/4
   /the-richest-americans-are-sitting-on-4-trillion-how-can-they-be-spurred
   -to-give-more-of-it-away.

16 *energy-processing units:* Thomas Gold, *The Deep Hot Biosphere* (New York:
    Springer, 1998), digital edition, https://www.amazon.com/Deep-Hot-Bio
    sphere-Fossil-Fuels/dp/0387985468.

    The fact that all living organisms need energy to stay alive is just Biol-
    ogy 101—but its significance didn't hit me until I read Thomas Gold's *The
    Deep Hot Biosphere* (an important book for an energy trader, because Gold
    argues that the earth holds far more oil than the fossil-fuel theory of oil's

origin suggests, whereas oil prices are predicated on a scarce supply of oil). Most fascinating to me, though, were the parts of the book about the origins of life from the simplest microbes to the most complex creatures, each relying on the chemical energy stored lower down the food chain. I latched onto the idea that I'm an energy-processing unit (EPU) every bit as much as a robot or a car is. That got me thinking about how calorically expensive it is to move our bodies, and how interesting it is that we build machines like planes that can move us great distances at high speeds—we are essentially EPUs that can build other EPUs. If you're looking for an intelligent, self-improving, replicating machine, it's here already, and it's called the human race.

2. INVEST IN EXPERIENCES

24 *"a time for work and a time for play"*: Aesop, "The Ants & the Grasshopper," in *The Aesop for Children* (Library of Congress), http://read.gov/aesop/052 .html.

27 *"investment in human capital"*: Gary S. Becker, "Human Capital," Library of Economics and Liberty, https://www.econlib.org/library/Enc/HumanCapi tal.html.

The economist Gary Becker identified health, along with education and training, among the most important investments in human capital.

33 *make your life what it is*: T. J. Carter and T. Gilovich, "I Am What I Do, Not What I Have: The Differential Centrality of Experiential and Material Purchases to the Self," *Journal of Personality and Social Psychology* 102 (2012): 1304–17, doi:10.1037/a0027407. https://cpb-us-e1.wpmucdn.com/blogs.cor nell.edu/dist/b/6819/files/2017/04/CarterGilo.JPSP_.12-14i5eu8.pdf.

Psychological research supports the idea that your experiences are closely tied to your sense of self, which helps explain why spending on experiences brings more happiness than spending on possessions. For example, when participants were able to conceive of something (like a TV) as either a possession or an experience, being experimentally prompted to think of it as an experience caused them to see the purchase as having greater overlap with themselves than thinking of it as a possession did.

36 *"the latte factor"*: David Bach, *Start Late, Finish Rich* (New York: Currency, 2006), https://www.amazon.com/dp/0767919475/ref=rdr_ext_tmb.

The term is a coinage of personal finance author David Bach, who registered it as a trademark and created a calculator to help you figure out how much you stand to gain over time from reducing small recurring expenses.

3. WHY DIE WITH ZERO?

43 *earners in the United States:* "Income Percentile by Age Calculator for the United States in 2018," DQYDJ.com, last modified May 31, 2019, https:// dqydj.com/income-percentile-by-age-calculator/.

approximately $48,911 per year: "Income Tax Calculator, Texas, USA," Neu-voo, https://neuvoo.com/tax-calculator/?iam=&salary=75000&from=year& region=Texas.

46 *"to zero by the date of death":* Michael D. Hurd, "Wealth Depletion and Life-Cycle Consumption by the Elderly," in *Topics in the Economics of Aging,* ed. David A. Wise (Chicago: University of Chicago Press, 1992), 136, https:// www.nber.org/chapters/c7101.pdf.

47 *"teach an old household new rules":* Hersh M. Shefrin and Richard H. Thaler, "The Behavioral Life-Cycle Hypothesis," in *Quasi Rational Economics,* ed. Richard H. Thaler (New York: Russell Sage Foundation, 1991), 114.

50 *long enough to enjoy that money:* Economists who study people's spend-ing and saving know that older people don't decumulate their savings fast enough, and the reasons they give match the two reasons I so often hear in conversations: "precautionary savings" (to address the fear of running out of money or not having enough for unforeseen expenses) and "the bequest mo-tive" (What about the kids?).

51 *various stages of their lives:* Jesse Bricker et al., "Table 2: Family Median and Mean Net Worth, by Selected Characteristics of Families, 2013 and 2016 Surveys," *Federal Reserve Bulletin* 103 (2017): 13, https://www.federalreserve .gov/publications/files/scf17.pdf.

52 *Employee Benefit Research Institute:* Sudipto Banerjee, "Asset Decumula-tion or Asset Preservation? What Guides Retirement Spending?," *Em-ployee Benefit Research Institute* issue brief 447 (2018), https://www.ebri.org /docs/default-source/ebri-issue-brief/ebri_ib_447_assetpreservation-3apr18 .pdf?sfvrsn=3d35342f_2.

54 *no-go years:* Michael K. Stein, *The Prosperous Retirement* (Boulder, Colo.: Emstco Press, 1998).

"stay close to home": Dan Healing, "How Much Money Will You Need Af-ter You Retire? Likely Less Than You Think," *Financial Post,* August 9, 2018, https://business.financialpost.com/personal-finance/retirement/how-much -money-should-you-have-left-when-you-die-likely-less-than-you-think.

56 *for those 75 and older:* "Table 1300: Age of Reference Person: Annual Expen-diture Means, Shares, Standard Errors, and Coefficients of Variation, Con-

sumer Expenditure Survey, 2017," U.S. Bureau of Labor Statistics, https://
www.bls.gov/cex/2017/combined/age.pdf.

more than half a million of its customers: Peter Finch, "The Myth of Steady
Retirement Spending, and Why Reality May Cost Less," *New York Times,*
November 29, 2018, https://www.nytimes.com/2018/11/29/business/retire
ment/retirement-spending-calculators.html.

57 *tend to save even more:* Shin-Yi Chou, Jin-Tan Liu, and James K. Hammitt,
"National Health Insurance and Precautionary Saving: Evidence from Taiwan," *Journal of Public Economics* 87 (2003): 1873–94, doi:10.1016/S0047
-2727(01)00205-5. When the government of Taiwan started offering health
insurance, people's savings declined.

still save too much: Michael G. Palumbo, "Uncertain Medical Expenses and
Precautionary Saving Near the End of the Life Cycle," *Review of Economic
Studies* 66 (1999): 395–421, doi:10.1111/1467-937X.00092, https://academic
.oup.com/restud/article-abstract/66/2/395/1563396.

59 *and other preventive care:* Anna Gorman, "Medical Plans Dangle Gift Cards
and Cash to Get Patients to Take Healthy Steps," *Los Angeles Times,* December 5, 2017, https://www.latimes.com/business/la-fi-medicaid-financial
-incentives-20171205-story.html.

paying premiums before you're 65: Ellen Stark, "5 Things You SHOULD
Know About Long-Term Care Insurance," *AARP Bulletin,* March 1, 2018,
https://www.aarp.org/caregiving/financial-legal/info-2018/long-term-care
-insurance-fd.html.

4. HOW TO SPEND YOUR MONEY (WITHOUT
ACTUALLY HITTING ZERO BEFORE YOU DIE)

65 *own at least some life insurance:* "Distribution of Life Insurance Owner-
ship in the United States in 2019," Statista, https://www.statista.com/statis-
tics/455614/life-insurance-ownership-usa/.

66 *"if you live a long time":* Ron Lieber, "The Simplest Annuity Explainer We
Could Write," *New York Times,* December 14, 2018, https://www.nytimes.
com/2018/12/14/your-money/annuity-explainer.html.

67 *"the annuity puzzle":* Richard H. Thaler, "The Annuity Puzzle," *New
York Times,* June 4, 2011, https://www.nytimes.com/2011/06/05/business/
economy/05view.html.

Dozens of scholarly papers have been written on this topic; if you want a simple explanation of the puzzle, including some possible answers, check out this "Economic View" column by recent Nobel laureate Richard Thaler.

72 *"leaving wealth behind":* Gary Becker, Kevin Murphy, and Tomas Philipson, "The Value of Life Near Its End and Terminal Care" (working paper, National Bureau of Economic Research, Washington, D.C., 2007), http://citeseerx.ist. psu.edu/viewdoc/download?doi=10.1.1.446.7983&rep=rep1&type=pdf.

74 *counts down the days:* "Final Countdown Timer," v. 1.8.2 (ThangBom LLC, 2013), iOS 11.0 or later, https://itunes.apple.com/us/app/final-countdown-timer/id916374469?mt=8.

The app is not specifically designed to count down to your expected death date—you can put in several different dates (deadlines, anniversaries, whatever you want) and watch the timer count down to all of them.

5. WHAT ABOUT THE KIDS?

80 *peaks at around 60:* Laura Feiveson and John Sabelhaus, "How Does Intergenerational Wealth Transmission Affect Wealth Concentration?," *FEDS Notes,* Board of Governors of the Federal Reserve System, June 1, 2018, doi:10.17016/2380-7172.2209. https://www.federalreserve.gov/econres/notes/feds-notes/how-does-intergenerational-wealth-transmission-affect-wealth-concentration-20180601.htm.

81 *plenty of financial resources:* Libby Kane, "Should You Give Your Kids Their Inheritance Before You Die?," *The Week,* August 21, 2013, https://theweek.com/articles/460943/should-give-kids-inheritance-before-die.

Virginia Colin struggled financially: Virginia Colin, interview by Marina Krakovsky, January 7, 2019.

83 *received an inheritance:* Edward N. Wolff and Maury Gittleman, "Inheritances and the Distribution of Wealth or Whatever Happened to the Great Inheritance Boom?," *Journal of Economic Inequality* 12, no. 4 (December 2014): 439–68, doi:10.1007/s10888-013-9261-8.

84 *intentional or not:* Marina Krakovsky, "The Inheritance Enigma," *Knowable Magazine,* February 12, 2019, https://www.knowablemagazine.org/article/society/2019/inheritance-enigma.

92 *lower levels of depression:* William J. Chopik and Robin S. Edelstein, "Retrospective Memories of Parental Care and Health from Mid- to Late Life," *Health Psychology* 38 (2019): 84–93, doi:10.1037/hea0000694.

94 *stressful jobs with long hours:* Carolyn J. Heinrich, "Parents' Employment and

Children's Wellbeing," *Future of Children* 24 (2014): 121–46, https://www
.jstor.org/stable/23723386.

99 *social benefits of education:* Jere R. Behrman and Nevzer Stacey, eds., *The Social Benefits of Education* (Ann Arbor: University of Michigan Press, 1997),
https://www.jstor.org/stable/10.3998/mpub.15129.

above 10 percent (per year): George Psacharopoulos and Harry Antony Pa-
trinos, "Returns to Investment in Education: A Decennial Review of the
Global Literature" (working paper, World Bank Group Education Global
Practice, Washington, D.C., April 2018), http://documents.worldbank.org/
curated/en/442521523465644318/pdf/WPS8402.pdf.

"their gifts will be used": Paul J. Jansen and David M. Katz, "For Nonprofits, Time Is Money," *McKinsey Quarterly,* February 2002, https://pacscen-
ter.stanford.edu/wp-content/uploads/2016/03/TimeIsMoney-Jansen_Katz_
McKinsey2002.pdf.

100 *investments in medical research:* Jonathan Grant and Martin J. Buxton,
"Economic Returns to Medical Research Funding," *BMJ Open* 8 (2018),
doi:10.1136/bmjopen-2018-022131.

6. BALANCE YOUR LIFE

104 *"middle-class family was taught to do":* Stephen J. Dubner and Steven D.
Levitt, "How to Think About Money, Choose Your Hometown, and Buy
an Electric Toothbrush," podcast transcript, *Freakonomics,* October 3, 2013,
http://freakonomics.com/2013/10/03/how-to-think-about-money-choose-
your-hometown-and-buy-an-electric-toothbrush-a-new-freakonomics-ra
dio-podcast-full-transcript/.

106 *called the 50-30-20 rule:* Elizabeth Warren and Amelia Warren Tyagi, *All Your
Worth: The Ultimate Lifetime Money Plan* (New York: Free Press, 2006), https://
www.amazon.com/All-Your-Worth-Ultimate-Lifetime/dp/0743269888.

111 *"major constraint to the oldest respondents":* Gyan Nyaupane, James T. Mc-
Cabe, and Kathleen Andereck, "Seniors' Travel Constraints: Stepwise Lo-
gistic Regression Analysis," *Tourism Analysis* 13 (2008): 341–54, https://asu.
pure.elsevier.com/en/publications/seniors-travel-constraints-stepwise-logis
tic-regression-analysis.

115 *your interests gradually narrow:* Robert M. Sapolsky, "Open Season," *New
Yorker,* March 30, 1998, https://www.newyorker.com/magazine/1998/03/30/
open-season-2.

122 *worked hard to achieve:* Rachel Honeyman, "Proof That 65 Is Never Too Late to Kickstart Your Fitness Journey," GMB Fitness, November 20, 2016, https://gmb.io/stephen-v/.

126 *before-and-after pictures on the Internet:* Valerie Cross, "Jaime and Matt Staples Win $150,000 Weight Loss Bet from Bill Perkins," *PokerNews,* March 23, 2018, https://www.pokernews.com/news/2018/03/jaime-staples-set-to-collect-on-150k-weight-loss-prop-bet-30300.htm.

127 *regardless of their income:* Ashley V. Whillans, Elizabeth W. Dunn, Paul Smeets, Rene Bekkers, and Michael I. Norton, "Buying Time Promotes Happiness," *Proceedings of the National Academy of Sciences* 114, no. 32 (August 8, 2017): 8523–27, doi:10.1073/pnas.1706541114.

131 *average stock market return:* J. B. Maverick, "What Is the Average Annual Return for the S&P 500?," *Investopedia,* last modified May 21, 2019, https://www.investopedia.com/ask/answers/042415/what-average-annual-return-sp-500.asp.

7. START TO TIME-BUCKET YOUR LIFE

139 *the two most common regrets:* Bronnie Ware, *The Top Five Regrets of Dying: A Life Transformed by the Dearly Departing* (Carlsbad, Calif.: Hay House, 2012), https://www.amazon.com/Top-Five-Regrets-Dying-Transformed/dp/140194065X.

141 *managed to squeeze more enjoyment:* Kristin Layous, Jaime Kurtz, Joseph Chancellor, and Sonja Lyubomirsky, "Reframing the Ordinary: Imagining Time As Scarce Increases Well-Being," *Journal of Positive Psychology* 13 (2018): 301–8, doi:10.1080/17439760.2017.1279210.

8. KNOW YOUR PEAK

155 *rates of homeownership:* Derick Moore, "Homeownership Remains Below 2006 Levels for All Age Groups," United States Census Bureau, August 13, 2018, https://www.census.gov/library/stories/2018/08/homeownership-by-age.html.

159 *value formula for an annuity:* PropertyMetrics, "Understanding Present Value Formulas," *PropertyMetrics* blog, July 10, 2018, https://www.property-metrics.com/blog/2018/07/10/present-value-formulas/.

162 *more money at the start of retirement:* Carolyn O'Hara, "How Much Money

Do I Need to Retire?," *AARP the Magazine,* https://www.aarp.org/work/re
tirement-planning/info-2015/nest-egg-retirement-amount.html.

164 *their full benefits:* Sarah Skidmore Sell, "'70 Is the New 65': Why More
Americans Expect to Retire Later," *Seattle Times,* May 8, 2018, https://www.
seattletimes.com/nation-world/nation/more-americans-expect-to-work-un
til-70-not-65-there-are-benefits/.

plan to work past 65: "When Do Americans Plan to Retire?," Pew Charitable Trusts, November 19, 2018, https://www.pewtrusts.org/en/research-and-
analysis/issue-briefs/2018/11/when-do-americans-plan-to-retire.

165 *forced out of their jobs:* Peter Gosselin, "If You're Over 50, Chances Are the
Decision to Leave a Job Won't Be Yours," *ProPublica,* last modified January
4, 2019, https://www.propublica.org/article/older-workers-united-states-
pushed-out-of-work-forced-retirement.

the most common retirement age: "Average Retirement Age in the United
States," DQYDJ.com, last modified May 31, 2019, https://dqydj.com/aver
age-retirement-age-in-the-united-states/.

as is the median: "Report on the Economic Well-Being of U.S. Households
in 2017," Board of Governors of the Federal Reserve System, last modified
June 19, 2018, https://www.federalreserve.gov/publications/2018-economic-
well-being-of-us-households-in-2017-retirement.htm.

170 *"laughing uproariously":* Anne Kates Smith, "Retirees, Go Ahead and Spend
a Little (More)," *Kiplinger's Personal Finance,* October 3, 2018, https://www.
kiplinger.com/article/spending/T031-C023-S002-how-frugal-retirement-
savers-can-spend-wisely.html.

171 *higher in some industries:* Government Accountability Office, "Older Workers: Phased Retirement Programs, Although Uncommon, Provide Flexibil-
ity for Workers and Employers," report to the Special Committee on Aging,
U.S. Senate, June 2017, https://www.gao.gov/products/GAO-17-536.

employees with in-demand skills: Stephen Miller, "Phased Retirement Gets
a Second Look," Society for Human Resource Management, July 28, 2017,
https://www.shrm.org/resourcesandtools/hr-topics/benefits/pages/phased-
retirement-challenges.aspx.

173 *reruns of* The Golden Girls*:* If you don't know that *Jeopardy* is a TV game
show or that *The Golden Girls* is a sitcom, chances are you haven't lived in
the United States for very long.

9. BE BOLD — NOT FOOLISH

182 *partner in his own firm:* "The Big Interview: 5 Minutes with . . . Jeff Cohen," *Chambers Associate,* n.d., https://www.chambers-associate.com/the-big-in terview/jeff-cohen-chunk-from-the-goonies-lawyer.

186 *positive memory dividends:* Kathleen D. Vohs, Jennifer L. Aaker, and Rhia Catapano, "It's Not Going to Be That Fun: Negative Experiences Can Add Meaning to Life," *Current Opinion in Psychology* 26 (2019): 11–14, doi:10.1016/j.copsyc.2018.04.014.

Illustration Credits

The net worth data used in the figures on pages 51, 116, 163, and 166 comes from the United States Federal Reserve, (2016), table 2. Data from Jesse Bricker et al., "Changes in U.S. Family Finances from 2013 to 2016: Evidence from the Survey of Consumer Finances." *Federal Reserve Bulletin* 103 (2017): 13. https://www.federal reserve.gov/publications/files/scf17.pdf.

The data used in the figure on page 81 comes from the Board of Governors of the Federal Reserve System (2018), figure 3. Data from Laura Feiveson and John Sabelhaus, "How Does Intergenerational Wealth Transmission Affect Wealth Concentration?" FEDS Notes. Board of Governors of the Federal Reserve System. June 1, 2018, doi:10.17016/2380-7172.2209. https://www.federalreserve.gov /econres/notes/feds-notes/how-does-intergenerational-wealth-transmission-affect -wealth-concentration-accessible-20180601.htm.

The data used in the figure on page 172 comes from Ann C. Foster, "Consumer Expenditures Vary by Age," *Beyond the Numbers* 4, No. 14 (December 2015), Bureau of Labor Statistics, https://www.bls.gov/opub/btn/volume-4/mobile/con sumer-expenditures-vary-by-age.htm.

Index